ILLUSTRATED TRANSPORT ENCYCLOPEDIA

Fantasy Cars

An A–Z of the world's best contemporary classics

ILLUSTRATED TRANSPORT ENCYCLOPEDIA

Fantasy Cars

An A–Z of the world's best contemporary classics

CHRIS REES

LORENZ BOOKS

This edition is published by Lorenz Books

Lorenz Books is an imprint of Anness Publishing Ltd
Hermes House, 88–89 Blackfriars Road, London SE1 8HA
tel. 020 7401 2077; fax 020 7633 9499; www.lorenzbooks.com; info@anness.com

© Anness Publishing Ltd 1999, 2004

UK agent: The Manning Partnership Ltd, 6 The Old Dairy, Melcombe Road, Bath BA2 3LR;
tel. 01225 478444; fax 01225 478440; sales@manning-partnership.co.uk

UK distributor: Grantham Book Services Ltd, Isaac Newton Way, Alma Park Industrial Estate, Grantham, Lincs NG31 9SD;
tel. 01476 541080; fax 01476 541061; orders@gbs.tbs-ltd.co.uk

North American agent/distributor: National Book Network, 4501 Forbes Boulevard, Suite 200, Lanham, MD 20706;
tel. 301 459 3366; fax 301 429 5746; www.nbnbooks.com

Australian agent/distributor: Pan Macmillan Australia, Level 18, St Martins Tower, 31 Market St, Sydney, NSW 2000;
tel. 1300 135 113; fax 1300 135 103; customer.service@macmillan.com.au

New Zealand agent/distributor: David Bateman Ltd, 30 Tarndale Grove, Off Bush Road, Albany, Auckland;
tel. (09) 415 7664; fax (09) 415 8892

Publisher: Joanna Lorenz
Editorial Director: Helen Sudell
Assistant Editor: Emma Gray
Designer: Alan Marshall
Production Controller: Lee Sargent
Editorial Reader: Hayley Kerr

Previously published as part of a larger compendium, *Encyclopedia of Dream Cars*

The Publishers would like to thank the individual car manufacturers and Classic and Sportscar magazine, Haymarket Specialist Motoring,
for supplying most of the pictures in the book. Additional pictures supplied by Beaulieu: p46TR, CL; P47BC; p106TR; P120 BL; p121TL;
p128TC, BR; p130TC, C, RC, BL, BC; p136TR; p139TC; p147CR
Key: T=TOP, C=CENTRE, B=BOTTOM, R=RIGHT, L=LEFT

1 3 5 7 9 10 8 6 4 2

CONTENTS

Introduction

The 1970s was a difficult time for motoring, with oil crises, escalating congestion, pollution issues and industrial troubles. Yet a true golden age of cars began at this time, reaching full bloom in the late 1980s and 90s, as cars became more rewarding to drive, leapt ahead in technical terms and grew in design appeal. What had simply been dreams on the part of drivers now became reality. The fantasy car was born.

One definition of the word fantasy is "a highly elaborate imaginative design or creation." This is the thread that joins all the cars you will find in this book. All of them are cars created by passionate enthusiasts to be the best, in design terms, in their fields. Yet fantasy does not mean far-fetched. The cars in this book are all machines that have won adulation in the real world, not far-out concept cars that you have no chance of ever driving. These cars are all meant to be driven.

These cars boast speed, inspire excitement, reward skilful driving and satisfy in the details of their design. We can all appreciate what makes a Ferrari or Lotus a fantasy car, but that doesn't mean that only exotic sports cars are fantasy cars. Brilliant design can also be fantasy. Ingenious packaging can be fantasy. Seemingly innocuous cars that are more than the sum of their parts can also be fantasy; this is what makes the classic car of our time.

This is the story of a new generation of classic cars, one that charts the progress of our own history and experience. This book is a celebration of that progression and a recognition of the value and importance of these fantasy cars in our lives.

ALFA ROMEO

■ ALFA ROMEO GT/GTV

This smart sports coupé was launched in
1974 as the Alfetta GT. It was based on
a shortened version of the Alfetta saloon
floorpan, so it shared its racing-inspired
rear-mounted gearbox. Perhaps the car's
best feature was its superbly clean

■ RIGHT *The 1980
GTV6 brought
fuel-injected power
to the Alfa, and
there was also a
major face-lift.*

ALFA ROMEO GT/GTV (1974–86)	
Engine	4/V-six-cylinder
Capacity	1570–2934cc
Power	109–186bhp
Transmission	5-speed
Top speed	111–140mph (179–225kph)
No. built	136,275

■ LEFT *All Alfa GT/GTV models handled
superbly, and the best of the bunch was this
late-model GTV6.*

■ ABOVE *For a coupé, the GTV was very
practical, with four full seats and a proper
opening tailgate.*

■ ABOVE *The 2.5-litre V-six engine in the
GTV6 delivered 160bhp – enough for a top
speed of 127mph (204 kph).*

styling by Giugiaro. This was also a very
practical car thanks to its hatchback
rear opening.

The interior was very distinctive: only
the rev counter (tachometer) was sited
in front of the driver. All the other
gauges were stacked in a central

binnacle. There was more room for people
than in most coupés in the GT class.

Initially, there was only one engine,
the Alfetta 1.8, but by 1976, 1.6 and
2.0-litre units were added, the latter
called GTV. There was even a very
potent turbocharged model, but this was

sold in tiny numbers (around 20). In
1980, the 2.0 GTV became the only
model sold and got a face-lift, featuring
larger bumpers and a more conventional
instrument layout.

The best GTV of all was undoubtedly
the GTV6 of 1980. Into the familiar
body Alfa Romeo fitted a fuel-injected
2.5-litre V-six engine. Performance was
now extremely high, and suspension
changes and a limited slip differential
made it handle superbly. Yet this was
not the quickest GTV of all: that honour
goes to the GTV 3.0 produced in Alfa
Romeo's South African factory. Like
other GTV models, this boasted
considerable success on the race-track,
as well as being a very satisfying car to
drive on the road. Today, it is the most
desirable of the classic GTV family.

■ ALFA ROMEO 164

Traditionally, Alfa Romeo produced rear-wheel-drive sporting cars and was generally most successful with its smaller saloons and coupés. Its track record with larger cars was not very good, the 1970 Montreal and 1979 Alfa 6 being complex, poor-selling, problem-ridden machines.

That all changed with the 164, the first Alfa to emerge following Fiat's 1986

take-over of the group. Not only was the 164 quite the most handsome saloon (sedan) car of its day – thanks to Pininfarina's master hand – but it had sharp front-wheel-drive handling and, most importantly of all, it was built up to a quality that rivalled Germany's best. The interiors looked as if they had been designed by an architect.

The floorpan was shared with three other cars: the Fiat Croma, Lancia Thema and Saab 9000. However, Alfa installed its own range of engines, which was always the marque's best feature. The range started with a two-litre Twin Spark (two spark plugs per cylinder) and culminated in a three-litre V-six. All engines were capable of reaching 125mph (201kph). The ultimate Q4 model had four-wheel drive, six speeds and a 230bhp Cloverleaf engine.

If there was one criticism of the 164, it was a tendency to suffer from torque-steer, which means pulling right or left

under acceleration. Alfa Romeo addressed the worst of the problem early on and also developed a Super version with longer body-coloured bumpers and chrome strips.

The 164 undoubtedly led a renaissance at Alfa Romeo, and re-establishing confidence in the marque. It left production in 1997 after a distinguished career.

■ FAR LEFT *Pininfarina's styling was widely admired for its crispness and distinctively Alfa Romeo character.*

■ LEFT *Pininfarina's extraordinary sculpted dash was a work of art, but the profusion of switches was criticized as confusing.*

ALFA ROMEO 164 (1987–97)	
Engine	4/V-six-cylinder
Capacity	1962–2959cc
Power	114–230bhp
Transmission	5/6-speed manual
Top speed	125–152mph (201–245kph)
No. built	248,278 (to end 1994)

■ BELOW *Technically, the 164 borrowed its floorpan from Fiat/Lancia, but added its own engine range and sports-tuned suspension.*

ALFA ROMEO

■ OPPOSITE *It was difficult to describe the SZ's stocky shape as beautiful. The Italian press affectionately called it "Il Mostro" – the monster.*

■ ALFA ROMEO SZ/RZ

Italians coined a new phrase to describe the amazing Alfa Romeo SZ: "Il Mostro", or The Monster, and it is easy to see why. In no way could the bodywork be described as handsome, but if you were looking to make a visual impact then this Alfa supercar was king. Although Alfa Romeo announced the birth of this amazing new model under its internal type designation of ES30, production cars were known as SZ.

The design house responsible for the SZ was Zagato, which has always had a strong association with Alfa Romeo. Zagato also produced the SZ for Alfa at its Milanese factory. The time it took for Zagato to develop and produce the SZ was a remarkably short two years. To

■ ABOVE *The striking SZ made its debut at the 1989 Geneva Motor Show where it created many headlines.*

■ LEFT *Even more desirable among Alfisti was the convertible RZ model, only 241 of which were made.*

3.0-litre V-six engine was given even more power thanks to integrated fuel injection/ignition systems, new camshafts and modified manifolding. Maximum power was now up to 207bhp.

Since the SZ weighed only 2822lb (1280kg), performance was deeply impressive: a top speed of over 152mph (245kph) and 0–62mph (0–100kph) in only seven seconds was quoted. The SZ was quite capable of handling all this

make the bodies, Zagato elected to use plastic composites (a mixture of thermosetting resins and glassfibre), mounted on a steel chassis. The result may have looked spectacularly ugly but it was surprisingly aerodynamic: its Cd (co-efficient of drag) figure of 0.30 was superior to that of many other cars.

Underneath that extraordinary coupé bodyshell was basically the mechanical package from the racing version of the Alfa Romeo 75, including its layout of longitudinal engine, rear transaxle and rear-wheel drive. The familiar Alfa

■ RIGHT *Underneath the exterior lay what was basically a racing car. This made the SZ feel very much like a circuit racer on the road.*

power thanks to its sophisticated suspension and asymmetric Pirelli P-Zero tyres. One interesting feature was hydraulic adjustment for the rear suspension, which was occasionally needed to overcome ramps and other obstructions because ground clearance was just 2.4in (6cm).

Inside, the Alfa 75 driver would have felt immediately at home, since the instruments and much of the switchgear came from this humble saloon (sedan). Luxury was not overlooked, though, as standard equipment included leather seats and electric windows.

At the end of 1992, the SZ was joined by an open-topped model called the RZ. This was more than just a roofless version of the SZ, as it incorporated a number of detail changes like a shorter front spoiler, thinner body panels, lower windscreen and reshaped sills. The chassis was considerably stiffened to compensate for the loss of the roof, and in consequence its weight went up by 220lb (100kg).

■ ABOVE *The three-litre V-six engine under the bonnet (hood) was familiar, but it was tweaked to give 207bhp – enough for a 150mph (241kph) top speed.*

■ ABOVE *Milan-based coachbuilder Zagato was responsible for the design and construction of the SZ.*

■ TOP *Perhaps the most flattering view is from the bird's eye.*

■ ABOVE *Luxurious leather seating contrasted with humble switchgear from the Alfa 75.*

ALFA ROMEO SZ/RZ (1989–94)	
Engine	V-six-cylinder
Capacity	2959cc
Power	207bhp @ 6200rpm
Transmission	5-speed
Top speed	152mph (245kph)
No. built	1,035/241

As planned, Zagato built just over 1000 examples of this exceptional sportscar, despite the fact that Alfa Romeo had received 1600 orders for the model, almost before it had even been seen by the public. An additional 241 copies of the RZ drop-top model were made in 1992–3. That means the SZ and RZ will always be among the rarest and most sought-after Alfa Romeos of all.

ALFA ROMEO

■ BELOW *The brand-new 1994 Alfa Spider was a startlingly fresh design created by Alfa Romeo's own Centro Stile in collaboration with Pininfarina.*

■ ALFA ROMEO SPIDER/GTV

The name Spider in Alfa Romeo's vocabulary dates right back to 1955, and the most famous incarnation of the model – the one driven by Dustin Hoffman in the film *The Graduate* – lasted 18 years in production. At the Paris Salon in September 1994, Alfa Romeo not only used the name for its exciting new roadster, it also revived another famous name from its past for a sister coupé model – GTV.

■ ABOVE *The classic Alfa Romeo Spider dynasty began back in 1966 and ended with this model, the Series 4, in 1994.*

The most striking feature of this new sportscar couple was the styling. The elegant and dramatic wedge shape recalled the 1991 Proteo show car and, if anything, the production cars' styling was even more adventurous than the

■ BELOW *If the Spider's handling was affected by its non-rigid bodyshell, the GTV was the opposite: taut, sure-footed and rewarding.*

show car's. A collaboration between Alfa Romeo's own Styling Centre and Pininfarina, the body made full play of the famous Alfa triangular grille. Other features included a plastic clam-shell bonnet (hood) with cut-outs for the high-intensity headlamps, an uncompromising rising belt-line indentation, tapering rear flanks and air intakes at the front, which were strongly reminiscent of past Alfas.

However, Alfa Romeo departed from its sportscar traditions by opting for front-wheel drive. If anyone was in doubt about how well the new car would handle with this set-up, a simple test drive dispelled all such concern. A unique multi-link rear suspension system allowed for a degree of rear-wheel steering, and in terms of steering response and grip around corners, the new Alfa could hardly be surpassed. There was a big difference between the ultimate abilities of the fixed-top GTV and the open Spider, though: the loss of rigidity in the body structure of the Spider let it down compared to the super-sharp GTV.

The GTV also differed from the Spider in another important respect: it had two seats in the rear, although they were so tiny that only very small children could ever be comfortable.

Performance was a definite strong suit. In Italy, there was a choice of three engines: a brand new 150bhp 2-litre 16V Twin Spark engine with variable valve timing, a 200bhp 2-litre V-six Turbo unit (GTV only) and a 192bhp 3-litre V-six. In Britain, only the Twin Spark engine was offered. All engines

■ ABOVE *Alfa's sportscar twins took a healthy share of the market, and have already become living classics.*

provided acceleration to match the sharp styling.

The cockpit was a triumph of clean design and classic feel: shrouded circular dials, sculpted steering wheel, pleasing upholstery and a profusion of Alfa Romeo badges. The driving position was unusually good for an Italian car, too.

For their price, there was little to touch Alfa's new sportscar twins in the desirability stakes. Perhaps it was the ineffable magic of the badge, or the strikingly bold shape, or the class-leading levels of handling and response. Whatever the appeal, the Spider and GTV have already passed into the realm of instant classics.

ALFA ROMEO SPIDER/GTV (1994)	
Engine	4/V-six cylinder
Capacity	1970–2959cc
Power	150–200bhp
Transmission	5-speed
Top speed	130–146mph (209–235kph)
No. built	Still in production

■ RIGHT *The front end of both cars was a triumph of styling: an adventurous clamshell bonnet with cut-outs for the high intensity projector headlamps.*

■ BELOW *The Spider was an exciting car to drive, even if some testers criticized the lack of rigidity in the bodyshell.*

■ ABOVE *The name GTV (last used in 1987) was revived for the fixed-head two-plus-two sister of the Spider, which was perhaps even more striking in its presence.*

ASTON MARTIN

■ ASTON MARTIN DB7

Aston Martin is part of a rich tradition of British coachbuilt sportscars. Its place is unique as a purveyor of brutally powerful, finely handcrafted, traditionally finished grand tourers. The "DB" dynasty of cars stretches back to 1947, the letters DB harking back to Sir David Brown, who owned Aston Martin from 1947 to 1972, and who helped design the DB7.

Ford became the new owner of Aston Martin in 1987. As well as giving the company the backing of a large

■ RIGHT *There is no doubt that the two Aston Martin DB7 models made an extremely strong pairing: elegant, powerful, luxurious, meticulously crafted and rich in character.*

■ BELOW *The most handsome car in the world? With the DB7, British designer Ian Callum created one of the great Aston Martin shapes.*

■ LEFT *The sumptuous interior reflected Aston's very British heritage and its tradition of hand-built quality: Connolly leather, tasteful British burr walnut, yet with plenty of modern electronics.*

organization, it instituted a new model programme, reviving the DB name on a new car that was designed to slot in below the existing Virage range. To develop this important newcomer, it turned to Tom Walkinshaw's TWR organization to do its best on the ageing platform of the Jaguar XJS.

The DB7 was the supremely elegant result. In style it was a classic, two-plus-two, front-engined, rear-wheel-drive car with superbly integrated, flowing lines designed by Ian Callum. Some were tempted to call it the most beautiful car in the world.

It was powered by a new 3.2-litre six-cylinder engine, which looked back to the past to boost its horse power: an Eaton supercharger helped it develop a

ASTON MARTIN DB7 (1994–)	
Engine	6-cylinder
Capacity	3239cc
Power	335bhp @ 5750rpm
Transmission	5-speed manual 4-speed auto
Top speed	155mph (249kph)
No. built	Still in production

■ RIGHT *The DB7 Volante immediately made an impact in sales terms, especially in America, boosting Aston Martin's production levels to an unprecedented high.*

massive 335bhp, enough to take the DB7 to a top speed of 155mph (249kph), with acceleration to match. Technically, the DB7 was very sophisticated, having sequential fuel injection, four-piston brakes and specially designed tyres.

This was a superb car to drive, sharp enough to cut it as a sportscar yet refined enough to make a convincing grand tourer. The chassis was pure magic.

Inside, rich Connolly leather upholstery was standard, as was traditional British burr walnut for the dashboard and centre console. Standard equipment included electric front-seat controls, air-conditioning, electric roof and Alpine sound system. There may not have been much room in the rear seats but at least they were there, and they could always double up as extra luggage space.

If the coupé looked seductive, the Volante convertible was the ultimate temptress in markets such as the US where up to 80 per cent of Aston Martin sales were of this model.

This was certainly not a cheap car, especially in Volante convertible form, and some people questioned whether it

was worth paying the extra for the DB7 when the Jaguar XK8, launched shortly after, looked and behaved so similarly and cost so much less. The Aston Martin was very much more exclusive, however, since a maximum of 700 per year could be built at the factory, and the badge carries a special set of qualities.

■ ABOVE *It may have had a mere six-cylinder engine, but supercharging and sophisticated fuel injection gave it 335bhp. The rest of the package was equally well engineered.*

■ ABOVE *Everyone who drove a DB7 was deeply impressed by its chassis, which provided keen handling, entertaining controllability and an accomplished ride.*

■ LEFT *A new Volante full convertible was presented ready for a 1996 launch. The hood (top) stacked under a tonneau cover in the British fashion.*

ASTON MARTIN

■ ASTON MARTIN VIRAGE

By 1988, Aston Martin had been relying on its mighty V-eight model for no less than 20 years, and it desperately needed a new car to tempt supercar owners. To design its car, it took the unusual step of asking several independent British car stylists to offer proposals, including Richard Oakes and Aston Martin veteran William Towns. The winner was John Heffernan's elegantly understated design, realized in aluminium by Aston Martin's skilled craftsmen.

The new Virage was unveiled at the 1988 Birmingham Motor Show and was greeted as the latest in a line of great British sportscars from the Newport Pagnell firm. It might have cost a six-figure sum, but its sumptuous specification, tremendous performance and hand-crafted quality were certainly appreciated by devotees.

■ ABOVE *Vast swathes of leather completely cloaked the cockpit; what it missed was covered with deep-pile carpets or polished wood.*

■ ABOVE *Even more muscle-bound was the later Vantage version, its twin supercharged engine boasting an incredible 557bhp.*

■ LEFT *For such an imposing, heavy and dimensionally grand car, the Virage managed to retain a certain elegance.*

■ ABOVE *When its V-eight engine kicked in, the Virage really flew. Its most impressive characteristic was almost limitless quantities of torque.*

ASTON MARTIN VIRAGE (1988–)	
Engine	V-eight-cylinder
Capacity	5340cc
Power	310–557bhp
Transmission	5/6-speed manual 4-speed auto
Top speed	160–186mph (257–299kph)
No. built	Still in production

In true Aston Martin tradition, each engine was hand-built and the name of the builder was placed on a plaque on the engine block. The familiar 5.3-litre V-eight engine was given a four-valves-per-cylinder head, developed by the American tuning company Callaway Engineering. Now power was up to 310bhp, and even more impressive was the torque figure of 340lb ft (461Nm (Newton metre)).

That all spiralled up to new heights with the pumped-up Vantage model of 1992. Twin superchargers raised the power figure to 557bhp and torque to just about the highest figure of any road car: no less than 550lb ft (745Nm) at 4000rpm. It was quicker than just about anything else on the road.

The most popular Virage model of all was the Volante, the convertible member of the family. Further choices were Shooting Brake (estate/station wagon) and Lagonda (four-door saloon/sedan) versions, a special 500bhp 6.3-litre engine and a version simply called V8 Coupé with Vantage-style wide bodywork and "only" 350bhp.

■ RIGHT *A mere 50 coupés was the plan, but a further run of convertibles brought the total of Aston Zagatos up to 89.*

■ ASTON MARTIN ZAGATO

All Aston Martins are rare but the 1986 Zagato was guaranteed to be one of the rarest of all. When Aston Martin released pictures and announced that it would be building only 50 cars at £70,000 ($117,810) apiece, buyers came

■ RIGHT *Aston Martin revived an old relationship with coachbuilder Zagato to create the fastest, most exciting production Aston yet in 1986.*

■ FAR RIGHT *There was only space for two passengers but they were treated to an Italian-styled cockpit trimmed to the highest standards.*

ASTON MARTIN ZAGATO (1986–90)	
Engine	V-eight-cylinder
Capacity	5340cc
Power	310–432bhp
Transmission	5-speed
Top speed	157–190mph (253–306kph)
No. built	89

rushing and all were pre-sold before any had been made. Speculators forced the price up as high as £500,000 ($841,500).

So what was all the fuss about? Italian coachbuilder Zagato had an illustrious history with Aston Martin stretching back to 1958, and this was to be a modern equivalent of the immortal DB4 Zagato. In addition to being a special-bodied Aston, it would be the company's

quickest ever car. An already mightily powerful Vantage V-eight engine was tuned even further to give over 430bhp, and Aston Martin quoted a top speed of 190mph or 306kph.

This was essentially a special-bodied, lightweight, short-wheelbase Aston Vantage with two seats and an Italian-designed interior. Zagato not only designed but also built the car. There was some concern that the finished article did not look much like the drawings that had convinced buyers to hand over deposits, but there was no doubting the brutal nature of the drive. Acceleration was explosive at 0–60mph (0–96kph) in under five seconds and handling was certainly more incisive than other Astons.

It was decided that the exclusivity of the coupé would not be harmed by adding a limited run of 25 Volante convertibles to the roster, and the

prototype drop-top was shown at Geneva in 1987. In fact 52 coupés and 37 Volantes were made in total, the last one being produced in 1990. Controversial it may have been, but it was also the ultimate in Aston exclusivity.

■ ABOVE *The performance was brutal. A top speed of 190mph (306kph) was claimed, and you could do 0–60mph (0–96kph) in under five seconds.*

AUDI

■ AUDI QUATTRO

The idea of four-wheel drive as an aid to fast road driving rather than pure off-roading may not have been new (Jensen introduced the FF supercar in 1966), but Audi certainly pioneered the art-form in the real world. The 1980 Quattro was the first mass-produced performance car to feature permanent four-wheel drive.

■ FAR LEFT *The Quattro Sport was a strict two-seater with a 300bhp engine – expensive and a very rare sight.*

■ LEFT *Safe and forgiving, the Audi Quattro became the handling benchmark of the 1980s.*

The four-wheel-drive system rewrote everyone's definition of handling limits. It certainly made it probably the safest car to be driving in wet or icy conditions. Reports in some journals even seemed to suggest that the Quattro was invincible around corners whatever the road conditions; in fact of course every car has its limits, and the Quattro's were simply much higher than other cars', but unfortunately dozens of owners found this out the hard way by asking too much of the car, and ending up in a ditch.

The body was based around the recently launched coupé, with suitably bulging wings and a deeper front spoiler. Audi was not above adding gimmicks to the package, notably a dubious digital talking dash.

Power was also very high thanks to a turbocharged 2.1-litre five-cylinder engine. There was mighty turbo lag (the time it took for the turbocharger to cut

■ LEFT *Not only was the Quattro grippy, it was very quick too, thanks to its five-cylinder turbo engine. This is a 1988 20V version with 220bhp.*

AUDI QUATTRO (1980–91)	
Engine	5-cylinder
Capacity	2144–2226cc
Power	200–220bhp
Transmission	5-speed
Top speed	135–142mph (217–228kph)
No. built	11,452

in), but when it did, the Quattro simply flew: 0–60mph (0–96kph) in 6.3 seconds was stunningly fast for 1980. Braking was criticized for having too much front bias, but Audi soon corrected this with standard anti-lock brakes.

This was not a cheap car by any standards: it cost more than a Jaguar XJS or Mercedes-Benz SL, but then it did offer a completely new class of driving experience.

■ OPPOSITE *The Quattro Sport was homologated for rallying and continued Audi's dominance in the sport for many years.*

■ BELOW *It was on slippery surfaces like snowbound mountains that the Quattro really shone, gripping the road where others wandered.*

The Quattro permanent (full-time) four wheel-drive system also turned the rally world upside-down. Audi swept the board with its newcomer, and very soon everyone recognized that they weren't going to win anything unless they, too, adopted an all-wheels-driven strategy.

Later models got a bigger engine and more power, and the ultimate Quattro was the short-wheelbase Sport model launched in 1983. This limited-production homologation (production-recognized) special had a 300bhp 20V engine and was capable of 155mph (249kph). At three times the price of a standard Quattro, it was strictly for rich would-be rallying stars.

When Audi announced that Quattro would soon be axed, there was an outcry from enthusiasts and the production run

■ ABOVE *The road-car interior was extremely well designed, if a little sombre.*

was extended, the model finally bowing out in 1991, after 11 years of service. For many people, this superb Audi was deserving of the title "car of the decade".

OTHER MAKES

■ AC

Thames Ditton-based AC started life in 1911 as Autocarriers and, post-war, AC progressed through ever-more powerful sportscars, culminating in the legendary V-eight-powered, Shelby-developed Cobra and the Frua-styled 428. By 1973, AC needed a new model and the ME3000, with its mid-mounted Ford V-six, was shown in 1973 but not actually produced until 1979, and then in tiny quantities. The project went to Scotland in 1984, and was modified to become the Ecosse, but ended in bankruptcy. Bryan Angliss's Autokraft revived the Cobra and in 1986 showed a new Ace model (scrapped by new owners Ford in 1987). Ford sold out again to Autokraft in 1992, and an all-new Ace model was produced. Today, AC produces the Ace and a new version of the Cobra called Superblower.

■ ABOVE *Because of its superior traction the Quattro was a runaway success in rallying, where it dispensed with the rough stuff and scored dozens of victories.*

■ AUTOBIANCHI

Part of the Fiat empire since 1955, by the 1970s Autobianchi was firmly established as the "character" wing of the small-car department with models like the 500 Giardinera and Fiat 127-based A112. In the 1980s, Autobianchi was allied to the Lancia brand, producing the Y10. When the Y10 was replaced in 1996, subsequent products were badged as Lancias, and the Autobianchi name sadly died.

■ AVANTI

Raymond Loewy's swoopy Avanti was produced by Studebaker for just two years (1963–4), but a private consortium took it over and continued to make it right up until the present day. The styling was very un-Detroit, the bodywork glassfibre, the interior very luxurious and the price exorbitant. Avantis have a small but fanatically loyal band of followers.

BENTLEY

■ BENTLEY CONTINENTAL/AZURE

In the 1950s, the name Continental represented the very pinnacle of superior transportation: with such a badge on your Bentley, you were assured of absolute opulence combined with effortless touring power, and everyone else could be assured that you were driving quite the most expensive car money could buy.

That was Bentley's golden age, at least in post-war terms. After the great Continentals were retired by the parent company, Rolls-Royce, Bentleys became merely badge-engineered versions of Rolls-Royce products. By the 1970s, Bentley represented a mere 5 per cent of

all Rolls-Royce group sales. A great name was being squandered.

Luckily, the management at Crewe realized this fact and began a steady renaissance of Bentley. First came the Mulsanne Turbo, basically a much more powerful version of the Rolls-Royce Silver Spirit, which also benefited from being less ostentatious.

■ ABOVE *A fabulously evocative interior with milled aluminium made the Continental T feel very special. Note the red starter button in the centre console.*

■ ABOVE *The addition of a T to the Continental name meant a complete transformation: fat wheels, short wheelbase, 400bhp engine – an upper-class hot rod.*

BENTLEY CONTINENTAL/AZURE (1991–)	
Engine	V-eight-cylinder
Capacity	6750cc
Power	385–400bhp
Transmission	4-speed auto
Top speed	155mph (249kph)
No. built	Still in production

■ BELOW *All the Bentley trademarks were present: an imposing gait, sporting demeanour and a large grille surmounted by a simple winged "B" badge.*

The sporting heritage of the Bentley badge deserved more, however, and in 1991 it got it. The Continental name was revived for a model that had no Rolls-Royce equivalent: here was a true-blood Bentley that lived up to the provenance of its name.

The new car was actually christened the Continental R, the R nominally referring to Roadholding. This was a handsome and imposing two-door coupé, some 17ft 6in (5.34 metres) long, 6ft 2in (1.88 metres) wide and 2.5 tonnes (2.46 tons) heavy. The extravagance of such an ample car was

■ OPPOSITE *Without a roof the Continental transmuted into the Azure. Pininfarina engineered the superb electric folding roof.*

■ RIGHT *Perhaps the R's handling was still a little barge-like compared with some rivals, but it was far better than previous Bentleys.*

flaunted at its Geneva Motor Show launch, as the show car was painted the brightest shade of red obtainable.

To pull all that bulk, Rolls-Royce engineers stayed with its familiar 6.75-litre V-eight and truck-derived Garrett turbocharging, in this form good for about 385bhp and a huge 553lb ft (750Nm) of torque. Transmitting this tidal wave of power through a GM four-speed automatic gearbox, the R was indecently fast: 0–60mph (0–96kph) in 6.1 seconds and a top speed of 155mph (249kph), or enough to despatch a well-driven Porsche.

Rolls-Royce called the new Continental "the finest sporting coupé in the world", and with some justification: despite its proportions, it handled respectably, rode very comfortably, cosseted the driver and passengers in the utmost luxury and sustained the most unerring ambience of serenity and superiority.

At £160,000 ($269,000) this was also, in 1991, the most expensive British car ever made, yet it sold better than any other model in the Bentley range. Bentley even saw fit to induce yet more from its superlative creation. First came the Continental S, with over 400bhp at its command. Then followed the Azure, the convertible version of the Continental, which was for some time the only car in which to be seen on the Côte d'Azur, justifying setting its owner back a cool £215,000 ($362,000).

The mighty Continental T is the most radical member of the Bentley family. Its wheelbase was shortened, its wheelarches were flared, and its wheels were massive five-spoke alloys. The interior was laced with milled aluminium. Delightfully, you had to press a big red button to start the engine, which now had no less than 590lb ft (800Nm) of torque to dig into, making it surely the world's most upper-class hot rod.

■ ABOVE *Nothing less than the renaissance of the Bentley marque was how many described the impact of the Continental R, the first specific new Bentley for three decades.*

■ ABOVE RIGHT *Costing a cool £215,000 ($362,000), the Azure was for the seriously wealthy only. The south of France was its natural habitat.*

■ RIGHT *The R had huge pace thanks to its turbocharged 6.75-litre V-eight engine. Naturally, the ride quality was superlative.*

BITTER

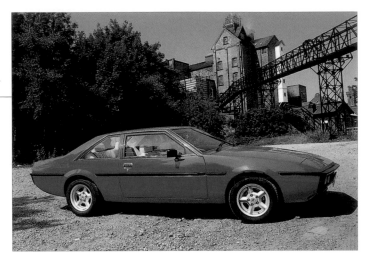

■ BITTER

German-born Erich Bitter was a race driver and car-accessories tycoon. He was smitten by two Opel CD prototypes presented in 1969 and 1970 and was so disappointed that Opel did not go into production that he managed to persuade the General Motors-owned company to hand the project over to him. Opel even helped him develop the car into production-ready form.

Since Bitter did not have the resources to set up his own factory, production began in 1971 at coachbuilders Baur of Stuttgart. An Opel Diplomat saloon (sedan) chassis was shortened and its suspension retuned for the lighter car, but otherwise the mechanics were left untouched, including GM's 5.4-litre V-eight engine.

This was a very handsome car, and definitely in the same league as Italian exotics. It could be ordered in any of 45 different colours, had a luxurious cabin trimmed by Baur and an Opel-sourced dashboard. It was certainly not a cheap car, costing almost as much as a Rolls-Royce, but its quality and dashing looks

persuaded many customers to flock to the hitherto unknown marque. Production got underway at the rate of about one car per week.

The big American-designed V-eight engine provided refined, torquey performance, making it ideally suited to a grand touring role, rather than an overtly sporting one. Handling was sharp but not in the same league as greats like Ferrari and Porsche.

Just as handsome as the CD was Bitter's next car, the SC. This was first shown in 1979 but took another two years to enter production. Again this used Opel parts – the newly launched Senator – and the coupé body was styled by Bitter himself. The 3.0-litre fuel-injected six-cylinder engine was more in keeping with the times than the the old GM V-eight, and the later Bitter-modified 3.9-litre version was even more suitable, having an extra 30bhp at

■ ABOVE *The proud badge of the Bitter CD, neat and effective like the car itself.*

■ RIGHT *The CD's styling was widely admired for its simplicity and good proportions. The elegance factor drew buyers by the dozen. Bitter's cabin used an Opel dashboard but was sumptuously trimmed by specialists Baur of Stuttgart.*

BITTER CD (1971–79)	
Engine	V-eight-cylinder
Capacity	5354cc
Power	230bhp @ 4700rpm
Transmission	3-speed auto
Top speed	129mph (208kph)
No. built	390

■ OPPOSITE *Perhaps even more handsome than the CD was the 1981 SC. Its three-box design was sharp and Italianate, often being compared with the Ferrari 400.*

210bhp. There was even the option of four-wheel drive, but only two cars were so equipped because of the expense.

Attractive cabriolet and long-wheelbase four-door versions were added in 1985, but this course proved far too ambitious: by then the company had overstretched itself and unfortunately production ended the following year; some 450 examples of the SC had been made.

■ BELOW LEFT *With a 6-cylinder fuel-injected engine, the SC was impressively rapid, but its best role was long-distance cruising.*

■ ABOVE *Although it used simple Opel mechanicals, the CD was a real driver's car: fast, assured and a comfortable cruiser.*

Bitter went on to develop other projects but so far these have remained in prototype form. The first was a convertible called the Rallye, based on the Opel Manta, but the impending demise of the Manta led to an evolution called the Type III. In production form, this would have had Opel Senator underpinnings, but sadly plans to market the car were dropped in 1992 amid continuing financial problems. Some years later, Bitter resurfaced with an imposing and elegant new four-door saloon (sedan) car, again based around Opel components, but its production fate remains in the balance.

■ ABOVE *Erich Bitter was the man behind the German-made Bitter CD. He cleverly persuaded Opel to release one of its prototypes for him to modify and manufacture.*

■ BELOW *The Bitter interior cleverly made use of Opel's parts bin in its own setting.*

■ RIGHT *Bitter faded from the scene in 1986, but it continued to exist, promoting new concept cars like the Type III. Isuzu was at one stage going to market this car but sadly that never happened.*

BMW

■ BMW M1

The motivation for the BMW M1, still BMW's one and only mid-engined supercar, came from racing and a new set of regulations. In the Group 5 Silhouette formula of 1976, BMW's aging CSL was losing out to Porsche's 935. To regain lost face, BMW needed a mid-engined chassis worthy of its magnificent twin-cam 3.5-litre straight-six engine: 400 examples would have to be built over a two-year period to qualify for the formula.

The M1 was conceived by BMW's Motorsport division. It was to be the first road-car application for BMW's superb M88 twin-cam straight-six engine. In Turbo Group 5 form it would give up to 700bhp, but for the road, BMW deemed

277bhp enough. Only the cast-iron bottom end came off the regular BMW production line; the M88 had a unique 24-valve twin-cam head with chain drive, a pukka forged-steel crank, race-style dry sump and longer connecting rods. It breathed through Kugelfischer-Bosch indirect injection.

The engine sat in-line and well down in the chassis behind the cockpit. Suspension was by unequal-length wishbones and coils, with huge vented disc brakes and rack-and-pinion

steering. There was a five-speed ZF transaxle to put the enormous power down on the road.

Initially, BMW turned to Lamborghini to sort out the details of the tubular steel chassis, build prototypes and assemble the 400 road cars required for homologation at the rate of two a week. Giugiaro's Ital Design was contracted to shape the body, taking inspiration from Paul Bracq's 1972 BMW Turbo show car. Prototypes were seen being tested

■ ABOVE *Thanks to its racing-derived 3.5-litre engine, the M1 was extremely rapid: a top speed of 161mph (259kph) was recorded by one magazine.*

■ RIGHT *BMW's M1 was its only true supercar, conceived as a machine that would be practical and reliable yet racing-car quick.*

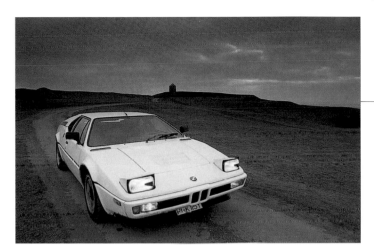

■ LEFT *There was no doubt that the M1 was an expensive supercar, but it was also one of the most exclusive ever made.*

■ BELOW *Clever aerodynamics played a large part in the success of the M1's shape. The black ducts are for engine cooling.*

around Sant'Agata in 1977, but by then Lamborghini was in deep financial trouble – and the M1 looked like a possible casualty. Lamborghini's government funding ran out, and delays caused BMW to snatch its M1 project back in April 1978, by which time seven prototypes had been built. It decided to transfer production to Baur, in Stuttgart.

Formally launched late in 1978, the M1 immediately fell foul of new Group 5 regulations that were its *raison d'être*. The revised rules said that 400 cars had to have been already sold to the public before a racing version could be used properly. By the time homologation was completed in 1981, the Group 5 M1 was already out of date, overweight and outclassed by a younger opposition.

If the M1 racer was never much more than a promising also-ran, the road car was always top-drawer material, not only fast (M1s were independently clocked at 161mph, or 259kph) but comfortable, refined, surprisingly frugal and beautifully built.

Handling was impeccable, and no mid-engined upper-echelon supercar rode so well or cruised so quietly. Disparate and convoluted as its cross-Europe design and manufacture had been, the values and quality behind this unfulfilled racer were always pure Munich. It bridged the gap between yesterday's dinosaur heavyweights and today's versatile supercars and is rightly regarded as one of the all-time classic supercars.

BMW M1 (1978–81)	
Engine	6-cylinder
Capacity	3453cc
Power	277bhp @ 6500rpm
Transmission	5-speed manual
Top speed	161mph (259kph)
No. built	450

■ ABOVE *The BMW "kidney" grille looked very purposeful on the aerodynamic nose of the M1. Pop-up headlamps improved airflow in the crucial nose section.*

■ ABOVE *Giugiaro designed the very simple and handsome shape, and it was built half in Italy and half in Germany in a very convoluted production process.*

BMW

■ BMW 6 SERIES

BMW has a strong reputation for producing powerful sporting coupés, its tradition stretching back to the earliest days. In the early 1970s, the BMW coupé ideal reached its zenith, the celebrated CSL becoming invincible on the track and accomplished on the road.

■ LEFT *The ultimate 6 Series was the 1983 M635CSi, fitted with a 286bhp M1 engine – good enough for a top speed of 158mph. Today, it is easily the most sought-after 6.*

■ ABOVE *Handsome, well-engineered, powerful and classy – the 6 Series was BMW's coupé for the 1980s.*

■ ABOVE *In typical BMW fashion, the dashboard was designed to curve around the driver. The cockpit was very spacious.*

BMW 6 SERIES (1976–89)	
Engine	6-cylinder
Capacity	2788–3453cc
Power	184–286bhp
Transmission	5-speed
Top speed	122–158mph (196–254kph)
No. built	80,361

By 1975, BMW needed to develop a successor, and the car earmarked to do this was the 630CS/633CSi, launched in March 1976. Compared to the old CS series, the 6 Series was larger, more cosseting and more expensive – a grand tourer, which was extremely good at its job of whisking along the autobahns, but not a true sporting car. The 1979 628CSi, with its even smaller engine, did little to enhance the image.

BMW attempted to remedy a lack of sporting feel by fitting its venerable 3453cc engine into the 6 Series in July 1978, creating the 635CSi. This engine was architecturally the same as that fitted to the M1, though it developed less power (218bhp). A far more sporting feel than the 633s was engendered by uprated dampers, springs and anti-roll bars and ventilated disc brakes.

It was really only a matter of time before BMW bit the bullet and fitted the full-house 24-valve M1 engine to create the M635CSi (M6 in the US). It shared the M1 specification very closely; with its light-alloy 24-valve head, twin overhead camshafts and central spark plugs, but owing to new induction and twin-pipe exhaust systems and the use of Bosch Motronic II digital engine electronics, it developed 9bhp more than the M1 engine. The new M635CSi was a real road burner.

The more powerful 6 Series BMWs were extremely good cars, notable for their fine handling, luxury, refinement and quality. The successor, the 8 Series, was in many ways less appealing.

■ RIGHT *Later 6 Series models got more power, sophisticated electronics and heightened levels of luxury.*

■ FAR RIGHT *While it was refined and rapid, the 6 Series was less sporting than the earlier CS series it replaced. It was really better suited to motorway driving.*

■ LEFT *BMW Technik was responsible for the short, neat shape of the Z1. A mere 8,093 examples were built.*

■ BMW Z1

The Z1 was a curiously un-BMW-like product, but enthusiasts everywhere were thankful that the company had the courage to put it into production. BMW was used to making drivers' cars, for sure, but its tendency was always toward the conservative. The Z1 was radical and highly specialized.

The project began life as a development mule for a new type of suspension for the BMW 3 Series. BMW Technik – the company's technical wing, mainly responsible for research and development – designed a body for it that was meant to show BMW was ahead of the game. It was displayed at the 1986 Paris Salon as a pure concept car, but the public response was so overwhelming that BMW boss Eberhard von Kuenheim gave the go-ahead for a production run.

After a series of modifications, the production Z1 was ready in 1988. Its basis was a steel monocoque chassis fitted with a composite thermoplastic body. Immense strength was engineered in by keeping very high sills, which raised a question about the doors; BMW solved this little conundrum by designing doors that dropped away into the sills, operated by electric motors –

■ ABOVE *The Z1 project began life as this development mule for new suspension systems, but the public reaction to its looks persuaded BMW to enter production.*

■ ABOVE *When the electric motors retracted the doors into the sills, getting in was an awkward exercise if the hood (top) was raised.*

great for fine-weather motoring. Aerodynamics were a strong point, and one novelty was a rear silencer (muffler), which also acted as an aerofoil.

The Z-axle rear suspension was the prototype of that for the forthcoming

BMW Z1 (1988–91)	
Engine	6-cylinder
Capacity	2494cc
Power	170bhp @ 5800rpm
Transmission	5-speed
Top speed	140mph (225kph)
No. built	8,093

3 Series, and gave great handling. The chassis could have handled more power than BMW gave it (the standard 325i engine was installed) but there was no questioning the fun factor. Equipment was deliberately sparse but the price tag was distinctly up-market: the Z1 cost the same as a BMW 735i, and was only ever a very limited-production prospect.

■ LEFT *The main party trick was doors that slid down into the high sills, bringing a new dimension to the term open-air motoring.*

BMW

■ BMW M3

In the 1970s and 1980s, BMW was the
most successful Touring Car racing
constructor, a remarkable feat since none
of its cars was a "homologation special"
– they were merely modified versions of
prosaic road cars. That all changed with
the M3, a legendary road car which also
swept the board in racing.

According to BMW's advertising, "M
is the most powerful letter in the world."

■ LEFT *The new-
shape 3 Series was
also made into an
M3 version with even
more power from a
six-cylinder engine,
and it had far fewer
rough edges.*

BMW M3 (1986–91)	
Engine	4-cylinder
Capacity	2302cc
Power	195–220bhp
Transmission	5-speed
Top speed	146–152mph (235–245kph)
No. built	17,969

M stood for Motorsport, a special
division within BMW, which was
responsible for racing and the
development of advanced road-car
projects. The M3 was actually based
on the current BMW 3 Series, but
Motorsport altered almost every
component on the car.

The bodywork became aggressive,
with its flared arches and spoilers, and
four individual bucket seats in the
interior. Under the body, the suspension
and braking were beefed up and the
gearbox had a race-style dog-leg first gear.

Most importantly of all, the M3 got a
very special engine: a large-capacity
four-cylinder unit fitted with a 16-valve
head modelled after the M1. With
200bhp available, it made the M3
outrageously quick. More than this, it
was endlessly entertaining to pilot along
twisty rounds, almost without vices. Very
quickly the M3 became a legend.

Limited-edition Evolution models
were even better, with enhanced
aerodynamics and, in ultimate Sport III
guise, a bigger 238bhp, 2.5-litre engine.
The most expensive M3 of all was the
Cabriolet, individually hand-built by
Motorsport staff.

When the old-shape 3 Series was
retired in favour of the smart new shape
car, there was of course an M3 version,
but it was ruthlessly efficient rather than
exciting. Many enthusiasts remember
the first-generation M3 with greater
affection, particularly its fabulously
controllable handling and raw character.

■ ABOVE *The interior of the Sport Evolution
model was covered in leather and race-style
suede and had very special seats. This was the
ultimate M3 model.*

■ ABOVE *The heart of the M3 was its four-
cylinder engine with a head derived from the
M1. Even in its least powerful incarnation, it
still had 195bhp on tap.*

■ BMW Z3

Not to be left out of the fashionable and burgeoning junior roadster market, BMW launched its Z3 range towards the end of 1995. The plan was certainly ambitious: to engineer a car from scratch and build it in a brand-new factory in Spartanburg, South Carolina, USA. Yet, it definitely paid off: even before the car's official launch in October 1995, posters advertising the new James Bond film, *Golden Eye*, showed exactly what the secret agent's new transport was – a Z3! Within 18 months, over 40,000 had been sold worldwide.

The new BMW roadster handled beautifully and made significant use of existing bottom-of-the-range BMW components, thus keeping the price of

■ LEFT *That BMW could successfully tackle the small sportscar market was proved with the Z3. This is the 1.9-litre model with a 140bhp engine.*

the "poverty" variant down to below £20,000 ($35,000). Where BMW's previous sportscar model (the 1980s Z1) had seemed crisp and forward-looking, many were underwhelmed by the Z3 shape, a not altogether happy mix of current BMW styling cues and half-hearted retro touches, such as the wing vents inspired by the classic 507 of the mid-50s. However, most buyers loved its sassy, overstyled shape.

The Z3 was stronger in many respects than competitors like the MGF and Mazda MX-5 Miata: it had a very solid shell, excellent build quality and great presence. Frugal but uninspired four-cylinder 1.8 and 1.9-litre engines were quickly joined by a powerful 2.8-litre six-cylinder and, in the spectacular M Roadster, the M3's 321bhp engine. This last was a real bargain supercar with beefed-up styling and a special interior

■ ABOVE *With a 2.8-litre engine, the Z3 became much more of an out-and-out sportscar. Note the wider alloy wheels for extra grip.*

BMW Z3 (1995–)	
Engine	4/6-cylinder
Capacity	1796–3201cc
Power	116–321bhp
Transmission	5-speed manual 4-speed auto
Top speed	115–155mph (185–249kph)
No. built	Still in production

■ ABOVE *The BMW roadster was built at a completely new factory in America, which could hardly keep up with demand.*

■ RIGHT *The Z3 was a real driver's car, as James Bond found out when he drove one in the film* Golden Eye. *The rear-wheel-drive chassis was impeccable.*

BRISTOL

■ BRISTOL 412 TO BLENHEIM

Bristol enthusiasts wept bitter tears when the 407 – Bristol's first Chrysler V-eight-powered model – hit the road in 1961. Out came the thoroughbred all-alloy straight-six engine – lovingly crafted by Bristol themselves – and in went an iron V-eight, shipped over in a wooden packing case from Canada (to evade import duty) and hitched up to an automatic transmission. To add insult to injury, it even had push-button controls.

It was the only way out for Bristol: the sweet little six, a mere 2.2 litres and 110bhp, was struggling with the weight of the opulent 406, and since Bristol could not afford to fund their own new 3.5-litre straight six, Detroit power was the only way to go.

It was the right decision. Bristol rode out every storm by keeping small, and

■ LEFT *In the early 1970s, Bristol's offering was the 411, a hand-built grand tourer, which essentially dated back to the 1950s.*

selling alloy-bodied, separate-chassied cars to a discreet and discerning few. The shape changed over the years, but the proportions – tall, slim and long – remained consistent right up to the latest Blenheim, still available today.

By 1975, the 411 was the latest incarnation of the Bristol ideal.

Radically different was the curious Zagato-styled 412 of 1975, a convertible coupé with big double roll-over bar. However, it still rode the classic 9ft 6in (2.89 metres) wheelbase chassis – which could be traced back to BMW's pre-war 327 coupé – and still had the 6.6-litre Chrysler V-eight engine.

BRISTOL 412 TO BLENHEIM (1975–)	
Engine	V-eight-cylinder
Capacity	5211–5665cc
Power	Not disclosed
Transmission	3/4-speed automatic
Top speed	120–140mph (193–225kph)
No. built	Not disclosed

■ LEFT *Zagato was responsible for the controversial styling of the 412, launched in 1975. This was a targa-topped convertible four-seater.*

■ OPPOSITE *All Bristols featured this hinging side panel, inspired by aerodynamics. On the other side was a panel for the spare wheel.*

■ LEFT *Bristol's traditions simply did not fade. This Brigand model, despite its turbocharging and alloy wheels, was very much in line with its long-standing heritage.*

■ BELOW *Many famous celebrities were attracted to the understated character of the Bristol, which was very much a car for the wealthy.*

In 1976, the 412 became a convertible saloon (sedan) with a standard hardtop, while the S2 of 1977 had a smaller 5.9-litre engine. The rapid 140mph (225kph) Beaufighter of 1980 had an American Rotomaster turbocharger, beefed-up gearbox and a restyled front-end, and remained in production until 1992.

The curious 603E and 603S of 1976–82 featured new styling on familiar hardware. They replaced the long-running 411, whose alloy body was basically that of the 406 of 1958. The short-lived E was a 5.2-litre "economy" model, while the S had the usual 5.9-litre engine. Both had cruise control, air-conditioning and the latest Torque-Flite automatic gearbox with long-striding "lock-up" top (a locking torque converter) and self-levelling suspension.

The Brigand and Britannia replaced the 603 in 1982. The Brigand was turbocharged and could sprint to 60mph (96kph) from rest in under six seconds and reach a 150mph (241kph) top speed. The cars ran on alloy wheels and featured new front and rear styling.

The Blenheim of 1993 had yet another new front- and rear-end restyle, but the basic shape was the familiar 603/Britannia body. Bristol claimed that only the roof and doors were retained, but much of the interior looked familiar from previous Bristols, notably the handsome binnacle and round white-on-black instruments.

The Blenheim was fitted with the latest fully managed and injected 5.9-litre Chrysler engine and four-speed automatic gearbox. There was no turbocharger this time, but economy was much better, and certainly the Blenheim made a consummate long-distance express for the wealthy enthusiast who wanted to be a little bit different – owners included Liam Gallagher, lead singer of the UK rock band Oasis, and Virgin business entrepreneur Sir Richard Branson.

■ LEFT *Traditional British luxury in the cockpit of this Britannia: leather, wood and Wilton carpeting.*

BUGATTI

■ BUGATTI EB110

Following the Second World War, Ettore Bugatti's fabulously engineered, but vastly expensive creations were at odds with the times, and production never really restarted. There were many attempts to revive the name but none was very convincing – until a man called Romano Artioli stepped into the arena. This canny Italian magnate managed to rekindle the Bugatti magic in spectacular fashion, but ultimately the dream proved overambitious and ended in bankruptcy.

The plan was grand: a state-of-the-art factory was built in northern Italy, industry greats were hired (including Paolo Stanzani as technical director and Marcello Gandini as designer – both of them effectively fired later on), and a brand-new V-twelve engine was created from scratch.

The new Bugatti EB110 was to be a superlative mid-engined supercar, the sort of car that Ettore would have been making if he were still alive. The EB110 name was chosen as a composite of Ettore Bugatti's initials and the fact that the car was to be launched on the 110th anniversary of his birth.

The aluminium-bodied Bugatti's styling (created by an Italian architect) was dramatic but controversial: the lines were hardly harmonious and the traditional Bugatti horseshoe grille looked almost farcically small on the car's nose. Inside, meanwhile, the level of finish was superb and equipment levels were generous, but space was severely limited.

Mechanically, the Bugatti was highly advanced. Its centrepiece was a

■ ABOVE *The new EB110 was launched at an incredibly lavish party in Paris. It attracted a huge amount of publicity.*

■ LEFT *The avant-garde new Bugatti factory in Italy was highly regarded.*

■ LEFT *This is the prototype workshop. Clearly visible is one of the amazing V-twelve engines, which were hand-built by Bugatti. Each unit developed at least 553bhp.*

■ ABOVE *Reviving the fabled Bugatti badge was always going to be a hard task. "EB" stands for Ettore Bugatti, the marque's founder.*

■ RIGHT *If the standard car seemed a bit dull to you, you could order this Supersport version with less weight, a rear spoiler, bigger wheels and no less than 611bhp and 221mph (356kph).*

V-twelve engine fitted with no less than four turbochargers and 60 valves, developing 553bhp. There was a six-speed gearbox mated to a four-wheel-drive system and suspension, which delivered handling akin to a grown-up Lancia Integrale. Bugatti claimed a top speed of 212mph (341kph) and stated that this was the fastest road car in the world; Jaguar with its XJ220 and McLaren with the F1 might have questioned this, but no one was in any doubt that the Bugatti was an extraordinarily fast and very capable machine.

By the time the EB110 was launched (at a lavish party in Paris in 1991), the supercar sales boom of the 1980s was already well and truly over. The list price was a walloping £285,000 ($486,000) and, if that all seemed a bit pale, Bugatti also developed a lightweight SS model with a 611bhp engine and up to 221mph (356kph) – total cost was an extra £50,000 ($93,000).

In the end, Artioli simply became too ambitious. First he bought up Lotus from General Motors in 1993, then he commissioned Ital Design to build a new four-door super saloon (sedan) called the EB112, but Ital Design stopped work on the project, claiming lack of payment. By 1995, Bugatti was bankrupt and its showcase factory lay tragically deserted. Unfortunately, it is not known exactly how many cars were built; Artioli claimed 154, including the one built for the German racing driver Michael Schumacher.

■ LEFT *Bugatti commissioned a second model, called the EB112, from Ital Design. This would have been an opulent limousine but production was prevented by Bugatti's liquidation.*

■ LEFT *The new Bugatti EB110 was in all respects an amazing car. Strikingly styled, enormously powerful and superb to drive, it fittingly revived the Bugatti name.*

BUGATTI EB110 (1991–95)	
Engine	V-twelve-cylinder
Capacity	3500cc
Power	553–611bhp
Transmission	6-speed
Top speed	212–221mph (341–356kph)
No. built	Not known

CATERHAM

CATERHAM 7

The basic design of the Caterham 7 can lay a strong claim to be the oldest still in production. Its origins stretch back to the 1957 Lotus 7, a car that engineering genius Colin Chapman said he "knocked up in a weekend". Lotus made the car for 15 years, while Graham Nearn's Caterham Cars sold them, often when everyone else had given up on it.

When Lotus decided to end production of the 7, Graham Nearn's special relationship with Colin Chapman enabled him to acquire the rights to make the car in 1973. Initially, Caterham Cars struggled to make the plastic-bodied Series 4 Lotus 7. Soon, however, it turned to the simpler and ultimately more purist aluminium-bodied Series 3.

In many ways, the 7's appeal lies precisely in what it does not have. There are no gadgets, no complicated electronics, no expensive compound-curved body panels. The 7 is fixed on one goal: providing the maximum driver enjoyment with the minimum of material. This was the very essence of Colin Chapman's committed crusade for light weight.

In construction, the 7 had a tubular steel chassis clothed in aluminium panels; only the nose cone and wings were made of glassfibre. The rear axle came from either Ford or Morris, and later Caterham devised its own de Dion rear-end.

For its engines, Caterham initially continued using Lotus's brilliant 126bhp, 1558cc Twin Cam, but eventually stocks ran out and it switched to Ford engines in a variety of states of tune: GT (84bhp), Sprint (110bhp) and Supersprint (135bhp). If you wanted more power you could go for a Cosworth BDA engine with up to 170bhp and, later, a Vauxhall 2.0-litre unit with 175bhp. From 1991, Caterham switched

■ RIGHT 7s were typically very stark affairs, but this cockpit shows that luxury need not be abandoned, with leather trim and a plethora of gauges.

■ FAR RIGHT Caterhams were usually powered by Ford-derived engines, but 1991 saw a switch to Rover power, of which this is an example.

■ LEFT There is no other car so focused as the Caterham 7. Developed from Colin Chapman's Lotus 7, it embodies speed, passion and sharp senses.

to Rover K-series engines: 1.4 (103bhp), 1.4 Supersport (128bhp), 1.6 (115bhp) and 1.6 Supersport (138bhp).

The ultimate 7 was, however, the JPE (which stood for Jonathan Palmer Evolution, after the Formula 1 driver who helped develop it). With its 250bhp race-spec engine, lack of windscreen, carbon-fibre wings, extreme light weight and phenomenal braking, this was a very fast car: it did 0–60mph (0–96kph) in under 3.5 seconds and could beat a Ferrari F40 to 100mph (161kph).

■ RIGHT *The sensation of piloting the 7 is unique. A simple journey to the shops feels like driving a lap around a racing circuit.*

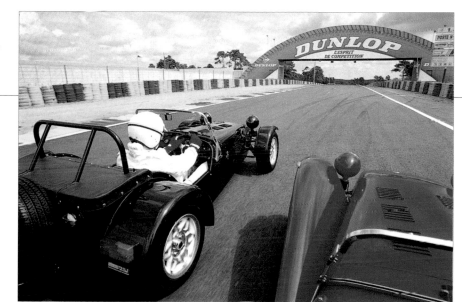

■ OPPOSITE *The image of the Super 7 was immortalized in the 1960s TV series The Prisoner, starring Patrick McGoohan. Caterham launched a special edition that encapsulated the spirit of "I am not a number, I am a free man!"*

Caterhams of whatever type offered more fun for your money than any other car. Most were bought in near-complete kit form with some components needing to be installed by the customer, which kept costs down and got round the need to Type Approve (legalize) the design. Most production was exported – Caterham received the Queen's Award for Export in 1993. Even today, over 40 years since the 7 appeared, the Caterham remains the absolute benchmark as far as handling and pure fun for the driver is concerned.

■ LEFT *Caterham promoted several one-make racing series involving 7s. This is action from the fastest class of all, the Vauxhall-powered Class A.*

CATERHAM 7 (1973–)	
Engine	4-cylinder
Capacity	1298–1998cc
Power	72–250bhp
Transmission	4/5/6-speed
Top speed	100–150mph (161–241kph)
No. built	Still in production

■ LEFT *The ultimate road-going 7 was the JPE, which stood for Jonathan Palmer Evolution, for the F1 driver helped develop this 250bhp thundering chariot. It once held the world record for the fastest-accelerating car.*

CATERHAM

■ CATERHAM 21

One guiding principle lay behind Caterham's custody of the 7 legend: you could do anything underneath the car to improve it, but the shape must remain untouched. With the 21, that philosophy was turned upside-down: here was a new model with a chassis based very closely on that of the 7 but with a totally new body. The 21 name indicated the

■ LEFT *For over 20 years the 7 never changed shape; then Caterham launched the 21, a bold new sportscar with a completely enveloping body.*

■ LEFT *This prototype was aluminium-bodied, an option that remained on the price lists after launch. The styling was by Iain Robertson.*

CATERHAM 21 (1996–)	
Engine	4-cylinder
Capacity	1588cc
Power	115–138bhp
Transmission	5/6-speed
Top speed	118–131mph (190–211kph)
No. built	Still in production

way Caterham was thinking: this was its vision of a car for the 21st century.

The plan to create an all-new Caterham began as an intention to make a mid-engined monocoque sportscar, but that would have been too ambitious. Instead, it was decided to create a new enveloping body over a modified 7 chassis. Journalist and designer Iain Robertson was called in to do the styling. For inspiration he turned to the classic racing Lotus XI, and his proposal looked exactly right: curvaceous, taut, recognizably British.

The interior architecture was adventurous and appealing, featuring an elegantly symmetrical design. The narrow cockpit was inherited from the 7, but the wide sills improved elbow room and leg room significantly. A narrow centre console housed switches and minor dials, the speedo and rev counter (tachometer) being sited directly in front of the driver.

Engineering the 21 posed a whole new set of problems for Caterham: never before had it been forced to deal with hinging doors and boot (trunk) lids, curved glass, sophisticated hoods or trimming the boot. It was getting all

■ RIGHT *In general, production cars had glassfibre bodywork and a painted finish. Demand for the new 21 was high, but production was limited to 200 per year.*

these details right that delayed the start of production for two years after the car's first showing in 1994.

The official launch at the October 1994 Birmingham Motor Show was spectacular: no one was expecting the car to be shown in gleamingly

■ ABOVE *On the road, the 21 was every bit as thrilling as the 7, but was far more practical, thanks to a locking boot, weather gear and doors.*

■ ABOVE *The lithe, taut shape drew from past Lotus models for its inspiration, but was undeniably modern as well.*

■ LEFT *The cockpit was a triumph of ergonomic design and beautiful shapes. Note the vertical central instrument cluster and very narrow seats.*

silver-polished aluminium. This would be an expensive option on the production 21, and most customers opted for the more viable choice of glassfibre. Prices were naturally higher than the 7, but the 21 was excellent value compared with rivals such as the Lotus Elise and Renault Sport Spider.

The valuable aluminium prototype was loaned to the press for early analysis, and testers were uniformly enthusiastic. This prototype was fitted with a Vauxhall JPE engine and six speed gearbox – a unique specification, since all production 21s would have Rover K series 1.6-litre engines or a very special version of the 1.8-litre MGF engine called the VHP (Very High Performance). Thanks to superior aerodynamics, the 293lb (648kg) 21 boasted a much higher top speed and far greater practicality than the 7, while inheriting all of the 7's handling finesse.

With an anticipated production volume of just 200 cars per year, the 21 will always be a rare beast, and its single-minded pursuit of driving pleasure will endear it to future generations of sportscar drivers.

■ ABOVE *The new badge reflected the company's assertion that this was a Caterham for the 21st century.*

■ LEFT *The first car was fitted with an extremely powerful Vauxhall JPE engine and was staggeringly fast. Production cars had Rover engines.*

CHEVROLET

■ LEFT *A convertible body option arrived in 1986 and was immediately very popular – there had not been an open-topped Corvette for over ten years.*

■ CHEVROLET CORVETTE

America's greatest sportscar – and for many years its only sportscar – is the Chevrolet Corvette. The name was born as long ago as 1953 when Detroit launched its plastic-bodied answer to the flood of European imports. A whole dynasty of 'Vettes followed on, up to the Stingray of the 1970s, which was as American as they come.

Then General Motors upped the stakes with a totally new generation Corvette launched in early 1983 as a 1984 model. Here was a thoroughly modern-looking sportscar that was still recognizably a 'Vette. The coupé shape was cleaner both aesthetically and aerodynamically and featured a hatchback and a removable roof panel.

The choice of glassfibre for the body remained, but the chassis was all new and the overhauled suspension used lightweight aluminium and even a plastic transverse spring.

The engine remained the faithful small-block Chevy V-eight, rated at 205bhp. It initially drove through a four-speed automatic transmission, but soon a four-speed manual was offered with no less than three overdrive ratios. Performance was a strong suit: 0–60mph (0–96kph) in 6.6 seconds was incredibly fast in anyone's book, and the roadholding was excellent.

A he-man clutch, tough steering and heavy brakes justified its reputation as a "muscle car". If there were criticisms to be made, they were minor: an awkward-to-view digital dash, harsh ride, irksome entry and snappy wet-weather handling.

Innovations in coming seasons included, from 1986, a new convertible and, from 1989, a six-speed gearbox and a three-position Selective Ride Control with adjustable shock damping.

■ LEFT *The ZR1 streaked away when the accelerator was depressed, and in addition to its dazzling acceleration was quite capable of reaching a top speed of 180mph (290kph).*

■ ABOVE *All Corvette interiors were luxuriously appointed and extremely well-equipped in the best American traditions.*

■ RIGHT *The Corvette as launched for the 1984 model year was available in one body style: a hatchback coupé with a removable roof panel.*

CHEVROLET CORVETTE (1984–96)	
Engine	V-eight-cylinder
Capacity	5727–5733cc
Power	205–411bhp
Transmission	4/6-speed manual 4-speed auto
Top speed	142–180mph (228–290kph)
No. built	Approx. 320,000

■ RIGHT *The new 1984 Corvette had quite a heritage to live up to: its eponymous brethren stretched all the way back to 1953. No one was in any doubt that the new 'Vette justified its billing.*

While the standard backbone chassis looked as if it came from Lotus, the ZR1 – then the ultimate Corvette of all – did actually owe much of its prowess to the English engineering firm (bought by GM in 1986). The 1990-model-year ZR1 was the new "King of the Hill", boasting a new, technically advanced LT5 375bhp engine that transformed the 'Vette into a crushing supercar: it could do 180mph (290kph) and reach 60mph (96kph) from rest in 4.5 seconds. Small wonder that this was the most expensive car in GM's history, retailing at £35,000 ($59,000). The ZR1's power went even higher in 1993, stretching to 411bhp. Ultimately, the King dropped off the price lists in 1996.

Meanwhile, the standard Corvette range continued, also with more power (305bhp). This generation of Corvettes was replaced by an all-new one in January 1997. The Corvette may never have been a huge seller or a big dollar-earner, but that wasn't the point: it was America's sportscar statement, and a remarkably good one. It's a fitting tribute that, thanks to over 40 years of continuous production, more Corvettes have been made than any other sportscar in the world.

■ LEFT *As America's only sportscar, the Corvette was quick in a straight line and much better around corners than virtually any other American car.*

■ BELOW *The heart of the new ZR1 was its quad-cam 32-valve LT5 V-eight engine, which developed a storming 375bhp.*

■ LEFT *Technically, the Corvette reiterated all the famous themes: a glassfibre body, powerful V-eight engine and muscle-car running gear. The chassis and suspension were all new, however.*

CHEVROLET

■ CHEVROLET CAMARO

The unprecedented success of Ford's Mustang sent rivals General Motors into a scurry of activity. However, in the two years it took to bring its answer to production, the great heyday of the "personal coupé" had already passed.

Its answer was the Chevrolet Camaro, and even General Motors could not have been disappointed when it sold 220,000 units in its first year. It was based on the uninspiring Chevrolet Nova body/chassis and mechanical package, but its strong suit was undoubtedly its classic "Coke bottle" styling by Bill Mitchell.

Both six-cylinder and V-eight engines were offered in various states of tune,

■ ABOVE *The fourth-generation Camaro arrived in 1993 as a smooth-looking coupé only; the convertible version did not appear until the following year.*

■ LEFT *The familiar Chevy "small block" V-eight engine powered most Camaros. This is the Z28 version with additional power, although in the 1970s emissions laws strangled power outputs across the board.*

■ ABOVE *One of the best of the "Coke bottle" first-generation Camaros was the Z28 edition, with its uprated engine, transmission, brakes and duck-tail rear spoiler.*

the most extreme being the SS (Super Sport) – of which 96,275 were built – and the RS (Rallye Sport) – 143,592 built. These have since become the most prized of all Camaros. As well as the more common coupé, Chevrolet also offered convertibles.

When it came to replacing the Camaro in 1970, General Motors took its

■ ABOVE *An all-new body shape arrived in 1970 and was essentially "right", lasting a full 11 years in production with no major changes.*

■ LEFT *The Camaro story kicked off in 1966, when General Motors came up with a car to rival the runaway success of the Ford Mustang.*

time and created a bespoke model (dedicated chassis) with monocoque construction instead of a separate frame. While the Mustang became bloated, then emasculated, the Camaro felt balanced in style and leaner, too. While the styling may have been less subtle than the first series (especially from the mid-1970s when the nose was reshaped to satisfy safety laws), the interior may have been cramped and there was no convertible option, it nevertheless struck a chord with the American buying public.

The 1970s Camaro was a big dollar earner for GM, selling almost two million examples. Overall it was nowhere near as powerful as the original series Camaro – even in Z28 form, the most desirable of 1970s Camaros. There was also a Pontiac clone called the Firebird with different engines and alternative front end styling.

■ FAR LEFT *As the years progressed, the Camaro kept up with the times. This 1991 RS model has a sculpted body, side skirts and modern sports wheels.*

■ LEFT *The Camaro badge always meant something special to American buyers.*

CHEVROLET CAMARO (1970–81)	
Engine	4/6/V-six-/V-eight-cylinder
Capacity	2475–6573cc
Power	90–360bhp
Transmission	3/4-speed auto 4/5-speed manual
Top speed	96–125mph (154–201kph)
No. built	1,811,973

■ RIGHT *The ultimate Camaro in its third generation was the Z28 edition, with a healthy increase in power.*

CITROËN

■ CITROËN CX

For most people the name Citroën
conjures up images of cars that are
quirky, eccentric, idiosyncratic – in
short, weird. More than any other model,
the CX is the one which firmly reinforces
these beliefs.

However, the CX is also one of the
most misunderstood and underrated cars
of all time. On the one hand, it is
remembered as one of the all-time greats
of motoring history; on the other, it has
been dismissed as an unreliable, rust-
infested, needlessly complex nightmare.

The CX was undoubtedly the last
great Citroën, the last car Citroën got to
design entirely in-house, before Peugeot
bought the company in 1974 and began
shaking its rod. Historically, it was the
replacement for the brilliant DS, in
production since 1955 and in dire need
of a modern successor.

What arrived shortly after was more
than just modern: it was positively
futuristic. Its GS- and SM-inspired
shape was not only one of the most
aerodynamic ever seen on a motor car, it
was also beautiful. Like the DS before it,

■ ABOVE *The cockpit looked like a mix
between French art and* Star Trek. *Note the
single-spoke steering wheel, rotating yellow
dials and spherical ash-tray.*

■ ABOVE *This is a 1985 GTI Turbo with a
168bhp engine providing near-sportscar levels
of performance. The CX was also extremely
impressive around corners.*

it bristled with advanced features. The
brilliant self-levelling hydropneumatic
suspension was there, tied in with the
braking and power-steering functions.
On all but the earliest CXs, the steering
also came with Vari-Power, Citroën's
patented weighted power assistance,
which altered the weighting of the
steering according to your speed.

Europe was impressed enough to
award the CX the Car of the Year trophy.
Its handling was assured, its ride
magical, its cruising ability ultra-
relaxed, its character unique. The
interior looked as if it had been sculpted
by an artist rather than designed for

CITROËN CX (1974–91)	
Engine	4-cylinder
Capacity	1985–2500cc
Power	66–168bhp
Transmission	4/5-speed manual C-Matic semi-auto 3-speed auto
Top speed	91–137mph (146–220kph)
No. built	1,042,300

■ LEFT *The extraordinary shape of the CX,
launched in 1974, was unique and way ahead
of its time.*

mass consumption, and the instruments, sited in a space-age binnacle, revolved themselves around stationary needles. Compared to the competition, the CX cleaned up – or should have done.

Where Citroën got it so badly wrong was in the build quality. In particular, there was a terminal rust problem every bit as bad as Alfa Romeo's during the 1970s, and it was this, more than anything, which crippled the CX. By the time Citroën had sorted the problem out – which took fully seven years – the CX already had a very bad name, made worse by the public's and the trade's suspicion of the eccentric hydraulic system.

History may well be kinder to the CX. In GTI Turbo form, it was stunningly quick and handled like a hot hatch. In long-wheelbase, luxury Prestige form it was the choice of French presidents. In eight-seater estate (station wagon) form, it was the most capacious European car around. Its replacement, the XM, looked just as individualistic as the CX, but it lost many of the features that made the CX unique.

■ ABOVE *The carrying capacity of the estate (station wagon) was enormous: it was Europe's most capacious car for the whole of its production life. Antique dealers loved them.*

■ RIGHT *Prestige was the name given to the long-wheelbase luxury model that whisked French presidents around Paris.*

■ ABOVE *From the rear the CX looked highly unconventional, with its concave rear window and rear wheels set closer together than the front pair.*

OTHER MAKES

■ CADILLAC

General Motors' premium brand is almost the American Rolls-Royce, with more glitz than any other marque. In the 1970s, it was producing huge, bloated cruisers like the Fleetwood and Eldorado. A significant move toward smaller cars was the 1976 Seville, famous for its 1980 "trunkback" restyle. The 1982 Cimarron (a jazzed-up Chevrolet) was a dead end, as was the Pininfarina-created Allante convertible. Cadillac's main business has always been selling luxury cars to the US establishment, a task which it continues to date, although Seville and recent Opel Calibra-based Catera have been respectable performance saloons (sedans).

■ CHRYSLER

The 1970s was a decade of crisis for America's Number Three car-maker. Ex-Ford man Lee Iacocca reversed the company's fortunes with government help. Chrysler was one of the first to down-size with its 1981 K-series (LeBaron, New Yorker and Laser). The most interesting models

in its line-up were the Laser and LeBaron coupés, plus the TC by Maserati, a high-spec soft-top with a Maserati-tweaked engine, which bombed spectacularly. After flirting with Maserati, Chrysler bought Lamborghini, but this relationship did not last long. Chrysler also invented the "people carrier" (minivan) phenomenon with the 1983 Voyager. Chrysler has pioneered many trends, including "cab-forward" design and the launch of the Viper and Prowler.

■ CLAN

The Clan Motor Company was formed by a group of former-Lotus men in Washington, County Durham. The 1971 Clan Crusader was a quirky little two-seater coupé of glassfibre monocoque construction with a Sunbeam Imp Sport engine. The car passed crash tests and a big factory was set up to produce large numbers of cars, but the economic crisis dragged the firm down in 1973. There was an attempt to revive a modified Clan in Northern Ireland in 1982, and the same operation produced the Alfasud-engined Clan Clover of 1986, but by 1987 it had ended in bankruptcy.

DE LOREAN

■ DE LOREAN

The John Z. De Lorean story is quite an epic. An ex-General Motors high flyer, De Lorean touted his idea for a dramatic but high-volume sportscar around several countries, in the search for financial support. The British government took the bait, offering grants and loans totalling more than £80 million ($134 million) if De Lorean would set up shop in economically disadvantaged Northern Ireland, and he accepted.

The ingredients of the De Lorean

■ BELOW *The use of gullwing doors was chosen for dramatic impact. In practice, the doors caused countless expensive production headaches.*

■ ABOVE *The V-six Peugeot/Renault engine sat in the tail under a large cover. Lotus designers helped sort out the handling challenges of such a layout.*

DMC-12 should have led to success: a chassis engineered by Lotus, a body styled by Giugiaro and a V-six engine from the Peugeot/Renault factory. Nor, given that it was only for the US market, was there anything wrong with its projected price of £15,000 (US $25,000).

But somehow the reality was different. De Lorean elected to use brushed stainless steel for the bodywork, which looked novel in the showroom but attracted dirt and scratches like chalk in the real world. The gullwing doors were another novelty, but they often leaked and, it was rumoured, could trap the car's occupants in a crash. Furthermore,

DE LOREAN (1980–82)	
Engine	V-six-cylinder
Capacity	2849cc
Power	145bhp @ 5500rpm
Transmission	5-speed
Top speed	130mph (209kph)
No. built	8,583

the quality of the early cars, built by an inexperienced workforce, was such that a second factory had to be opened in Los Angeles to rebuild them. Despite the effort of Lotus, the rear-mounted engine

■ ABOVE *After only a brief two-year existence, the De Lorean fluttered out amid financial crisis and scandal.*

layout never delivered anything better than indifferent handling. De Lorean announced massive production targets, but only 8,583 cars were built between the car's launch in 1980 and the collapse of the DeLorean Motor Company in 1982.

Thereafter it was controversy all the way: financial irregularities came to light and John De Lorean was arrested, but cleared, on drug-trafficking charges. The De Lorean is now something of a cult car with its own following of devotees.

DE TOMASO

■ **DE TOMASO PANTERA**

Elvis Presley shot his Pantera when it wouldn't start, and that is undoubtedly how many other owners felt about this enigmatic but slightly dodgy supercar.

Alejandro De Tomaso, an Argentinian tycoon who settled in Italy, built his first car, the Cortina-engined Vallelunga, in 1963. It flopped, and while his second effort, the Mangusta, was fast and beautiful, it quickly got a reputation for evil handling.

With the 1970 Pantera, De Tomaso was determined to get it right – and start making some money, too. He struck a deal with Ford of North America whereby they got his Ghia coachbuilding firm (hence the Ghia badge on today's Escorts and Fiestas) in return for selling his new car – powered by a 5.8-litre Ford V-eight engine – through their dealers in the US. It proved a sharp move as 4000 Panteras were unloaded on unsuspecting Americans before Ford shut the door on imports in 1974, beleaguered by complaints about build quality, rust and overheating.

The Pantera was fast in a straight line, topping 160mph (257kph), and with that mid-mounted engine the handling was copy-book stuff. It was practical, too: smash an engine in a Pantera and there

was no need to take out a second mortgage to replace it because it was just a big, dumb Ford V-eight as found in millions of lumbering American saloons (sedans).

The model lasted into the mid-90s, its image progressively cheapened by boy racerish spoilers and stickers and ever-fatter tyres. De Tomaso, however, had rather lost interest in the car that bore his name in the 1970s when he acquired several new business toys to play with, including Maserati and Innocenti.

■ ABOVE *In GTS form its massive spoiler, fattened wheel arches and prominent decals were so loud they were almost deafening.*

DE TOMASO PANTERA (1970–95)	
Engine	V-eight-cylinder
Capacity	4942–5763cc
Power	247–350bhp
Transmission	5-speed manual, 3-speed automatic
Top speed	150–160mph (241–257kph)
No. built	10,000

■ BELOW *Later Panteras became more rounded in profile, although no more subtle in style. The model stayed in production for an amazing 25 years.*

■ ABOVE *Classic 1970s themes in the interior: lots of chrome-ringed gauges, black-stitched trim and sports-style seats.*

■ LEFT *The relatively obscure Italian De Tomaso name won widespread fame with the Pantera, which was distributed in America by Ford.*

DODGE

■ DODGE VIPER

For decades, America's sportscar tradition hung on one sole car, the Chevrolet Corvette. By the end of the 1980s, however, Chrysler had come through its troubled times and was healthy enough to produce a new American sportscar legend.

When it was first shown at the 1989 Detroit Show, the Dodge Viper RT/10 stunned the crowds. The phrase "AC Cobra for the '90s" was bandied about at the show, and the impression was reinforced by the involvement of Carroll Shelby, the legendary creator of the Cobra, as a consultant. Chrysler

■ ABOVE *Viper was a fitting name for a car that recalled the glory years of the Shelby AC Cobra. Indeed, Carroll Shelby was even involved in the Viper's creation.*

executives displayed it as a concept car, and such was the public reaction that Team Viper was formed to turn dream into production reality, a process that took only 30 months.

The Viper was an amazing machine in all respects. Its plastic bodywork was pure machismo, a bristling contortion of muscular curves and suggestive ducting. There was no roof – except for a tent-like piece of vinyl and side curtains, which were supplied for use in the event of a shower. Just in case you got caught out, the interior was trimmed in waterproof materials. There were no exterior door handles, and the Flash Gordon three-spoke rear wheels were no less than 13-in (33-cm) wide.

The concept car had a truck-derived V-ten engine fitted and, in production form, Lamborghini made some changes, such as switching the block to aluminium rather than iron and giving it a bright-red head. But it remained

■ ABOVE *With its 8-litre V-ten engine, the Dodge Viper was a monster performer. It needed all of its 13-in (33-cm) wide wheels to rein in its 400bhp.*

distinctly low-tech: two valves per cylinder, hydraulic lifters, long pushrods. 400bhp may have been mightily impressive but the truck-like torque curve, peaking at 450lb ft (610Nm), was awe-inspiring. It didn't seem to matter that the engine note was rather subdued.

Acceleration was ballistic: 0–60mph (0–96kph) in 4.5 seconds.

DODGE VIPER (1992–)	
Engine	V-ten-cylinder
Capacity	7990cc
Power	400–455bhp
Transmission	6-speed
Top speed	165–180mph (265–290kph)
No. built	Still in production

■ LEFT *Viper owners usually drove their cars open-topped, but a special "double bubble" hardtop was developed in case you had to go out in rain.*

The Viper was one of the first cars to be fitted with a six-speed gearbox, but that was more to help fuel economy than to encourage stick-shifting: you could exceed 100mph (161kph) in sixth without going over 2000rpm, and still be turning just 3250rpm when you reached 165mph (265kph).

Perhaps the best thing about the Viper was its price: at £30,000 ($50,000) this was a supercar that many could afford, even though its impracticalities made it strictly a fair-weather fun car.

If you wanted more practicality, then Dodge offered just that with the Viper GTS coupé, shown in 1993 but not produced until 1996. This was more than a roof-up roadster, though: just about everything on it was changed. If you opened up the hatchback you had enough room for golf clubs, and you could even power-wind the glass windows: now the Viper had luxury and practicality as well as drop-dead good looks and gargantuan power.

OTHER MAKES

■ DAEWOO

Formed in 1967, Korean-based Daewoo has already become one of the world's great industrial giants. Cars form only a strand of its empire and began as licence-built products of General Motors, such as the Opel Rekord. By the 1980s, it was starting to modify GM's designs for the home market and then began an impressive export operation. The first car engineered by Daewoo was the 1997 Lanos, partly designed by newly acquired operations in Britain and Germany.

■ DAF

For many years the Dutch motor industry was DAF. In 1975, it was bought by Volvo and its existing range of small cars was rebadged Volvo, while a new model in the pipeline emerged as the Volvo 343. DAF's main contribution to the motoring world was its continuously variable transmission by rubber bands. DAF still exists as the factory where the Volvo S40 and Mitsubishi Carisma are made.

■ DAIHATSU

One of Japan's second grade of car-makers, Daihatsu has always specialized in small cars. It had the distinction of being the first Japanese marque to be exported to Europe (in 1965). In the 1980s, it became the leading maker of micro-class cars, and its Mira model was the best-selling car in Japan.

■ DAIMLER

Daimler, one of Britain's pioneering car names, was best known for its limousines (favoured by royalty) and for its sporting saloons (sedans). However this proud company came under Jaguar's control in 1960. Daimler's impressive V-eight engine continued in production until 1969, but by 1964 Daimlers had become essentially badge-engineered Jaguars with fluted grilles and occasionally more luxurious trim, which remains the position today, although Jaguar preserves its identity. The last model unique to Daimler was the darling of mayors across Britain, the DS420 limousine, which survived until 1992.

■ BELOW *The Viper's brawny shape began life as a show car, but public adulation brought it to production. Its burgeoning curves, massive wheels and side-exit exhausts were throwbacks to the muscle-car era.*

FERRARI

■ FERRARI
BERLINETTA BOXER

The immortal Boxer was Ferrari's first attempt at a flagship mid-engined model, though its history can be traced back to the 250LM Road Berlinetta, a road version of the 250LM racer, while some see the weird three-seater, centrally steered 365P show car of 1966 as its true spiritual father.

It was not until 1968, with the beautiful P6 show car, that Ferrari's favoured couturier Pininfarina really began to think aloud – and clearly – about the swoopy wedge profile of Maranello's supercar for the 70s, built to challenge the Lamborghini Miura and take over from the front-engined Daytona. Pininfarina's stylists started with a "big Dino" look, then flirted with the radical wedge influence of the 512 Modulo and futuristic 512S Berlinetta. Eventually, they settled on the elegant simplicity of the final production car, announced, prematurely, at Turin in 1971: production did not actually begin until 1973.

Under the big alloy engine cover was a new aluminium 4.4-litre four-cam

■ ABOVE *Ferrari owners are fanatical about their cars, and the Boxer inspired a new kind of loyalty. For many, this was the best car in the world.*

flat-twelve engine, descended from the 1500c 512 Formula 1 car of 1960. Breathing through four triple-choke (throat) Weber carburettors, it was for many the best engine in production, combining searing punch with pin-sharp throttle response and spine-tingling sound effects. Top speed was quoted as 188mph (302kph) – though no independent source confirmed it – 0–60mph (0–96kph) came up in 5.2 seconds.

To save space, the five-speed transaxle was tucked up under the engine, alongside the sump, all hung in an exotic multi-tube frame with a central

FERRARI BERLINETTA BOXER (1973–84)	
Engine	12-cylinder
Capacity	4390–4823cc
Power	340–360bhp
Transmission	5-speed manual
Top speed	175–188mph (282–302kph)
No. built	2,323

■ LEFT *Later cars had a 5-litre twelve-cylinder engine, which was more tractable in everyday use.*

■ OPPOSITE *As Ferrari's first-ever mid-engined flagship, the Berlinetta Boxer was always going to be a classic, and its Pininfarina-styled shape is one of the all-time greats.*

■ LEFT *With radical bodywork modifications, the 512 BB made a fearsome circuit racing machine.*

■ RIGHT *The Boxer's dart-like profile was extremely aerodynamic and unfussy. Note the long black cooling ducts over the mid-mounted engine.*

■ RIGHT *Subtle flowing lines combined with great presence. The rear end was surprisingly compact because the gearbox was mounted underneath the "flat 12" Boxer engine.*

the rear brakes, differently vented engine lid and four tail lights, not six.

The final incarnation of the Boxer was the 512i BB with Bosch K-Jetronic injection, which hacked an alarming 20bhp off the quoted power output but improved tractability and emissions. Production ended in 1984, making way for the controversially styled Testarossa. Ferrari built 2323 Boxers: 387 of the 365 model, 929 of the 512 and 1007 of the 512i.

steel monocoque around the passenger cell. Though the low-slung flat "boxer" configuration had the advantage of a low centre of gravity and better aerodynamics, the 365GT 4BB had a definite rear weight bias, with 56 per cent of its total weight over the rear wheels. At the limit, the handling could be a little ragged, and the Boxer certainly never had the cornering finesse of its arch rival, the Lamborghini Countach. The interior was finished in high-quality leather, and most cars came with air conditioning.

The five-litre 512 BB took over in 1976: its bigger bore engine, now with dry-sump lubrication, produced no extra power but 10 per cent more torque. A 512 could be spotted by its front spoiler, wider rear tyres, side air vents to cool

■ ABOVE *In its day, this was probably the fastest production car in the world. It was also*

fabulously sharp to drive, boasting instant throttle responses and tenacious handling.

FERRARI

■ FERRARI 308GTB/328GTB

With the authority of a "proper" Ferrari badge – the previous 246 Dino had been marketed as a Fiat – the 308GTB was announced at the Paris show in 1975, supplementing the Bertone-styled four-seater 308GT4. It also marked a return to Pininfarina as Ferrari's favoured stylist with a classically aggressive coupé that displayed little in the way of unnecessary ornament. That it changed so little in 13 years of production says much for its elegant purity. A strict two-seater, the 308GTB reverted to the 92in wheelbase of the V-six Dino, but

borrowed the tubular-steel chassis and uncompromised double wishbone suspension of the GT4. The large vented and servo-assisted (power) disc brakes made light work of the 1270kg (2800lb)

■ LEFT *Few cars of the 1970s had as much poise and balance as the GTB around corners. The mid-engined layout and V-eight engine combined to make this one of the best drivers' cars of all time.*

GTB, but with 3.5 turns lock-to-lock, the rack-and-pinion steering was not startlingly fast.

Mechanically, the car was almost identical to the GT4, producing 255bhp from a dry-sump version of the strident four-cam V-eight with twin distributors, an oil cooler and transistorized ignition. Rational toothed-belt drive for the camshafts hinted at the influence of Fiat, who were paying the bills. The engine was mounted transversely amidships ahead of the rear wheels, with the five-speed transaxle and limited slip diff tucked in behind it. Running a modest 8.8:1 compression ratio, the five-bearing unit took in fuel and air through four Weber carburettors.

■ ABOVE *The circular tail lamps were a real Ferrari/Pininfarina hallmark, distinguishing the already elegant shape.*

■ RIGHT *As a replacement for the classic Dino, the 308GTB was a brilliant effort. It had all the hallmarks of a classic Ferrari, and yet was the marque's entry-level model.*

■ ABOVE *Ferrari were not averse to making the driving environment luxurious as well as sporty, as the beautifully trimmed leather and electric switchgear show.*

■ LEFT *Pininfarina's devastatingly simple, uncluttered bodywork brought the 308GTB instant recognition as one of the design greats.*

■ BELOW *With the name GTS, the targa-topped "spider" version was extremely popular in hotter climates. Not recommended in the snow, though.*

The first cars had glassfibre bodywork, but after 18 months this was abandoned for more traditional steel body construction – adding 250lb (113kg) and the promise of rust problems for future owners. The Americans in particular lapped up the 308, particularly the targa-topped GTS model, which consistently outstripped sales of the closed car by a huge margin.

A significant change was Bosch Digiplex fuel injection (first seen on Ferrari's Mondial), which brought cleaner running but milder performance, as peak power tumbled to just 214bhp for the 1981 GTBi. Within 18 months, the Quattrovalvole (four-valve) model raised power to a healthy 240bhp with an accompanying increase in torque. With subtly bespoilered front and rear to prolong its shelf life, the QV's performance returned to its earlier pre-injection levels.

The final incarnation of this body shape was the 1985 328, bored and stroked to give 3185cc and 270bhp for a top speed of 160mph (257kph). Ferrari claimed that build quality was better and the handling sharper.

Some Ferrari experts tend to think of the 308GTB/GTS as the Ferrari for the common man, which comparatively it is: almost 20,000 were built between 1975 and 1989, of which 1637 came to Britain, making it one of the most successful Ferraris ever in that market. Its exceptional qualities confer it genuine classic status.

■ RIGHT *In ultimate 328 guise, the "baby" Ferrari was even quicker, boasting 270bhp from a 3.2-litre engine.*

■ BELOW *V-eight power for the 308 meant four camshafts, transistorized ignition, a dry sump and 255bhp. Later units gained fuel injection.*

FERRARI 308/328 GTB/GTS (1975–89)	
Engine	V-eight-cylinder
Capacity	2926–3185cc
Power	214–270bhp
Transmission	5-speed manual
Top speed	140–160mph (225–257kph)
No. built	19,555

FERRARI

■ FERRARI TESTAROSSA

There is something magical about the word *Testarossa*, a name that Ferrari has used since the 1950s. All it means is "redhead", and it refers to the colour of the cylinder head on the engine, but the name has acquired a mythical status by association.

The 1984 Testarossa was the successor to the great Berlinetta Boxer, and duplicated much of its specification on the same chassis, but the new car was much more than a rebodied Boxer. The famous 5.0-litre flat-twelve engine was given completely revised cylinder heads with four valves per cylinder (and naturally painted red!), with the result that power rose to 390bhp and flexibility was enhanced. Ferrari also used high-tech nickel-alloy to prevent heat damage to the valves.

■ LEFT *From the rear, the tremendous width was emphasized. It gave the car fantastic presence but made manoeuvring a rather fraught experience.*

■ BELOW LEFT *The 12-cylinder engine's red-painted cylinder head gave the Testarossa its name (Italian for "redhead"), and it was the automotive equivalent of war-paint applied before going into battle.*

■ BELOW RIGHT *Thanks to its side-mounted radiators, the straked cooling side ducts became a distinctive hallmark of the model.*

While the Boxer always had front-mounted radiators, the Testarossa switched to rear-mounted cooling, just ahead of the rear wheels. This dictated a new styling trait in the form of extremely wide rear wings punctured by dramatic horizontal strakes, which began in the doors. Pininfarina was responsible for the shape of the body. It was undeniably spectacular from any angle – especially the low, wide rear – but some questioned its audacity after the classically understated Boxer.

To save weight, the bodywork was all aluminium (except the roof and doors) and Pininfarina's wind tunnel confirmed the slipperiness and inherent down-force of the shape. The trade-off of having such a wide body (it was 78in (198cm) across) was that manoeuvring the car proved difficult, and visibility was very poor. This more than anything affected just how fast you could safely pilot the Testarossa.

In other respects Ferrari's new mid-engined top-of-the-range supercar was everything it should be. The engine sounded superb, the cabin was comfortable, the controls were light and – most importantly of all – this was an

■ OPPOSITE *The Testarossa recalled the glory years of Ferrari's Formula 1 effort. The 1984 Testarossa also recalled F1 themes with its mid-engined layout and squat stance.*

■ RIGHT *The final incarnation of the Testarossa series was the F512M of 1994-96. The most notable visible change was the cowled headlamps, but extra power also boosted the top speed to over 200mph (322kph).*

extremely fast car to drive. It could do the 0–60mph (0–96kph) sprint in 5.5 seconds and would keep on going to 180mph (290kph). Responses were always delicate, and the handling was rewarding.

In January 1992, the Testarossa was renamed 512 TR and revised extensively, the aim being to reclaim from Lamborghini's Diablo its title as the fastest car around. The TR name echoed the fact that this was essentially still a Testarossa, and only the new 348-style nose and larger wheels were very different.

Much more happened under the skin: more power (428bhp), lower ride height, better gearbox and improved suspension. The cabin was heavily revised, too. In short, the 512 TR was the best – and fastest – supercar in production.

The final evolution of the redhead was the F512M of 1994. This reflected Ferrari's preferred F prefix, while the M stood for "Modificata". Power went up by another 13bhp, so that its top speed now approached 200mph (322kph) and 0–60mph (0–96kph) came up in under five seconds. Other changes included cowled headlamps, bonnet (hood) ducts, new turbine wheels, restyled interior and classic round tail lights.

FERRARI TESTAROSSA (1984–96)	
Engine	12-cylinder
Capacity	4943cc
Power	390–441bhp
Transmission	5-speed manual
Top speed	180–200mph (290–322kph)
No. built	n/a

■ LEFT *In 1992 the Testarossa was renamed 512 TR after a minor restyle and a boost in power, from 390bhp to 428bhp, making it the fastest car in production.*

■ BELOW *Pininfarina's lines were widely admired – and copied – in the 1980s.*

FERRARI

▪ FERRARI F40

In the 1980s, Ferrari extended the boundaries of road-car performance with cars such as the Testarossa and the limited-production 288 GTO. Even considering these and other supercars, nothing came close to matching the F40, one of the greatest Ferraris of all time.

Enzo Ferrari proposed celebrating 40 years of his marque with a very special project that would combine race and road car traits in one machine. The Ferrari board agreed, and the F40, with bodywork by Pininfarina, was brought to production in just 12 months, helped by

the fact that it was based on the platform of the 1984–87 288 GTO.

The underlying goal during the F40's development was weight reduction. To this end, the body made innovative use of composite materials, which were claimed to be 20 per cent lighter than conventional metals. This priority also

meant the interior was utterly devoid of carpets and door trim. Ferrari certainly succeeded in its goal, since the F40 weighed in at just 2425lb (1099kg).

For power, Ferrari developed the 288 GTO V-eight to become a 3.0-litre twin-turbocharged beast. With sequential ignition and injection, silver/cadmium conrod bushes and nicasil-coated liners, the engine was capable of 478bhp – and up to 200bhp more if you wanted to go racing.

The performance figures spoke for themselves: a top speed of 201mph (323kph), 0–60mph (0–96kph) in 3.9 seconds and 0–124mph (0–200kph) in 12 seconds flat. This was far and away the quickest machine on the road when production began in 1988, almost a year after its debut. It was also the fastest road car Ferrari had ever built.

In character, the F40 was demanding to drive but not overly difficult, while it was hugely tractable yet superbly balanced in handling terms. The fact

▪ ABOVE *The F40 really looked like a racing car from the rear, and indeed many owners used their F40 in competition. The shape of the rear wing was widely copied by other designers.*

FERRARI F40 (1988–92)	
Engine	V-eight-cylinder
Capacity	2936cc
Power	478bhp @ 7000rpm
Transmission	5-speed manual
Top speed	201mph (323kph)
No. built	1,311

▪ LEFT *Features such as three-piece wheels, racing brakes, removable rear bodywork and soft fuel tanks (cells) hinted at racing origins.*

■ OPPOSITE *The inspiration for the F40 was a celebration of the 40th anniversary of Ferrari, and it was undoubtedly the best, and most audacious, car Enzo Ferrari had ever produced.*

■ ABOVE *The magic F40 sigil (seal) said it all. This ultra-rare Ferrari is bound to go down in history as one of the all-time greats.*

■ LEFT *With so much power going to the rear wheels – even with their massively wide tyres – burn-outs like this were almost inevitable at racing circuits.*

that the cockpit was sparsely trimmed was a positive point, and the sight of raw carbon fibre and exposed tubing was a delight, not a penance. It meant that being in an F40 was an extremely noisy experience but given the sound – as close to a racing engine as you could get – that was also part of what made the F40 experience so unique.

Considering its intended role as a dual-purpose road/race car, the F40 came with numerous competition features such as Group C brakes, three-piece wheels and bag fuel tanks (cells) ahead of the rear wheels.

It was very focused and technically advanced, but not the technological *tour de force* that the Porsche 959 was. Rather it was a car for the dedicated enthusiast, everything being directed towards making it faster and more precise. The fact that many owners successfully took their £163,000 ($275,000) F40 racing proved the point.

■ RIGHT *It may only have had three litres, but the V-eight engine was twin turbo-charged and provided with very special innards. The result was a 478bhp power output in standard road-going tune.*

■ ABOVE *The ultra-lightweight F40 was numbingly fast, and very close to a true racing car in feel and in the demands made on the driver. With a top speed of 201mph (323 kph), it was also the fastest Ferrari yet made.*

FERRARI

FERRARI F50

When the time came for Ferrari engineers to build a new flagship in the mid-1990s, the brief was simple and uncompromising: take our 1990 Formula 1 racer (the 641/2) and transform it into a street-legal 200mph (322kph) road car. Enter, in March 1995, the F50, the spiritual successor to the F40 and certainly the most potent road car yet made by Ferrari.

Clothed in a flat-bottomed Pininfarina body that recalled Ferrari's sports racers of the early 70s, it was easily the wildest road car Ferrari had ever built. With such headline-making performance figures, pundits made immediate comparisons with McLaren's stunning F1. It was understandable but in reality these were two very different cars: where the F1's designers pursued refinement and build quality as well as ultimate performance, the F50 – a shade slower than the bigger-engined and lighter McLaren – was more of a raw sportscar created to give its owner Formula 1 sensations on the road.

■ LEFT *Cowled projector headlamps and deep cooling ducts reminiscent of the Ford GT40 dominated the low, wide front of the F50.*

■ LEFT *It may not have had the stripped-out racer feel of the F40, but the F50's very simple cockpit was based on an ethos of comfort and light weight, as evidenced by the leather-covered carbon-fibre seats.*

The F50 nevertheless proved a surprisingly easy car to drive with a superb six-speed gearbox, reasonable ride (despite the rock-hard computerized damping and massive 335/30 ZR 18 tyres) and a user-friendly engine. Then there was the small matter of price: at £330,000 ($555,000) the

■ ABOVE *The V-twelve engine was essentially a Ferrari Formula 1 unit from 1990. Producing 521bhp, it was the closest a road-car driver could get to the sound and feel of an F1 car.*

■ LEFT *Pininfarina's stylists pulled another design classic. Despite the tight parameters supplied by Ferrari, the shape felt just right.*

■ ABOVE *The liquid-crystal instrument display was inspired by Formula 1 experience. There was even a "black box" flight recorder on board.*

■ LEFT *Everything was derived from racing, including the brakes, titanium uprights, ball joints and inboard pushrod/rocker-arm suspension.*

F50 was hardly cheap but still about half the cost of the British McLaren.

Boasting 521bhp from its Formula 1-derived five-valves-per-cylinder V-twelve engine, the F50 could do 64mph (103kph) in first, 112mph (180kph) in second, 124mph (194kph) in third, 138mph (222kph) in fourth, 160mph (275kph) in fifth and 202mph (325kph) in sixth. The handling was more forgiving than the F40 despite the extra speed, with superb non-assisted steering giving little kick-back but masterly precision.

With the iron crank-cased engine mounted rigidly to the chassis – and the rear wishbones attached to the gearbox – the noise was incredible, both in volume and quality, but nobody was complaining about that. In fact, chain rather than gear drive for the quad overhead camshafts meant less noise than the Formula 1 unit, while producing a smooth

idle and lower peak revs: 8500rpm instead of 14,000. Titanium connecting rods gave the unit high-rev strength.

Like the F1 car it was derived from, the F50 used proper inboard coil springs operated by pushrods and rocker arms, although, to make room for two people's feet, the front-end spring/damper units were transverse

rather than longitudinal. With titanium uprights and magnesium wheels, not to mention all-metal ball joints, it was no wonder the F50 steered with such precision. The F50 was to be much rarer than Ferrari's previous flagship hypercar, the F40: the company decreed that only 349 would be built, compared with 1311 F40s.

FERRARI F50 (1995–97)	
Engine	V-twelve-cylinder
Capacity	4968cc
Power	521bhp @ 8500rpm
Transmission	6-speed manual
Top speed	202mph (325kph)
No. built	349

■ RIGHT *An extremely neat hardtop could be fitted in poor weather, although the noise with the top on was simply deafening.*

FERRARI

■ ABOVE *Understated simplicity was the theme of the styling, from the mono-colour circular tail lamps to the lack of spoilers.*

■ ABOVE *A typically functional yet elegant and comfortable interior from Ferrari. Note the hallmark metal gear-lever gate.*

■ FERRARI 348/F355

When it came to replacing the noble and long-running 328, Ferrari was forced by tougher crash regulations to expand the size of its new entry-level car, called the 348tb. It also decided to fit the familiar V-eight engine longitudinally rather than transversely as before; the overall length was greater but the engine could now be sited a full 5in (12.7cm) lower down in the chassis.

The lower centre of gravity and stiffer chassis transformed the mid-engined Ferrari's handling from merely superb to deeply impressive. On-the-limit manoeuvres could be accomplished without fear of sudden tail-end break-away, yet it was at all times thrillingly rewarding to drive.

The engine was expanded to 3.4 litres and almost 300bhp, allowing for the expected levels of Ferrari forward thrust. Although the engine pointed front-to-rear, the gearbox was mounted transversely – hence the "t" in the name. Naturally, Pininfarina was called

■ LEFT *With the 348, Ferrari created a genuine masterpiece, especially in dynamic terms. Its low centre of gravity and ultra-rigid chassis produced a handling gem.*

upon to shape the 348 and it did another superb job. Testarossa-style side strakes endowed the otherwise subtle bodywork with a distinctly Ferrari character. A more spacious interior made life much easier, too. As well as the fixed-head tb, there was also a ts model with a removable targa roof and a full Spider

soft-top. In 1994, the 348 was updated to become the F355. At the heart of the newcomer was an expanded quad-cam five-valves-per-cylinder 3.5-litre V-eight. With up to 381bhp on tap, this supremely characterful power-plant delivered even more blistering performance: 183mph (0–294kph) top speed and 0–60mph (0–96kph) in 4.8 seconds. In-gear acceleration was optimized by a six-speed gearbox.

FERRARI 348/F355 (1989–)	
Engine	V-eight-cylinder
Capacity	3405–3495cc
Power	296–381bhp
Transmission	5/6-speed manual
Top speed	171–183mph (275–294kph)
No. built	Still in production

■ LEFT *The full range of 348 models encompassed the tb (coupé), ts (targa) and Spider (full convertible). This series was the most popular Ferrari had yet made.*

■ FERRARI 550 MARANELLO

Maranello is the northern Italian home of Ferrari, and it is fitting that at least one model should bear its name. Ferrari chose it in 1996 for its first new front-engined two-seater since the 365 GTB/4 Daytona, which was launched 28 years previously in 1968.

What could have caused such an about-face following its predecessor, the mid-engined F512M? The answer is that a front-engined car broadened Ferrari's range and made it very much more practical than the old F512M.

In terms of ancestry, the 550 was most closely related to the 456GT, a four-seater Ferrari Grand Tourer launched in 1992. It shared its basic V-twelve engine and suspension layout. Apart from the very special F50, the Maranello slotted in as the company's quickest car, claimed to reach 199mph (320kph) and to do the 0–60mph (0–96kph) sprint in 4.3 seconds.

It was a lot more refined than previous Ferraris, but that was again a reflection of the times. On Ferrari's fabled Fiorano test track, the new 550 proved to be 3.2 seconds a lap quicker

than the model it replaced. Perhaps the 550's greatest strength was that it felt so capable and refined: the world's fastest grand tourer, perhaps.

Some observers felt Pininfarina's styling lacked any real finesse. Good points were the elegant glass house, the subtle hump in the rear wings, the classic circular tail lamps; the real disappointments were the fussy

■ LEFT *550 Maranello was the evocative name, steeped in Ferrari lore, that was given to the replacement for the F512M. It marked the birth of a new ethos at Ferrari.*

■ ABOVE *Perhaps this was not one of the great Ferrari shapes, but the 550 found instant acceptance as a very rapid, more user-friendly Ferrari.*

FERRARI 550 MARANELLO (1996–)

Engine	V-twelve-cylinder
Capacity	5474cc
Power	484bhp @ 7000rpm
Transmission	6-speed manual
Top speed	199mph (320kph)
No. built	Still in production

front-end, the un-Ferrari-like shape and unhappy kicked-up tail.

At £145,000 ($244,000) the 550 cost over 50 per cent more than the dynamically more enthralling F355. In truth, the new Ferrari had a different sort of appeal: this was a tool as much for arriving at a destination feeling relaxed as for the sheer experience of driving.

■ FAR LEFT *Where the 550 differed radically from previous range-topping Ferraris was in its front-mounted engine. Note the superbly profiled aerodynamics of the undertray.*

■ LEFT *The 550 lapped Ferrari's Fiorano test track over three seconds faster than the F512M, thanks to a 484bhp V-twelve engine that was capable of powering it to a top speed of nearly 200mph (322 kph).*

FIAT

■ FIAT X1/9

The Fiat X1/9 is historic for this single fact: it brought mid-engined handling sophistication, previously reserved for exotica like Lamborghini and Ferrari, to a mass audience. Launched to rapturous praise from the world's motoring press in 1972, it was, like its predecessor, the Fiat 850 Spider, destined to sell in large numbers, especially in North America.

Bertone's razor-edged styling incorporated a nifty removable targa roof panel, stored in the front boot (trunk) when not in use. Pop-up headlights were also a novelty for the time.

Initially fitted with a 1290cc four-cylinder 85bhp single overhead-camshaft engine and four-speed gearbox from the Fiat 128 Rallye, the X1/9 was adequately brisk, with a top speed of 110mph (177kph) and a 0–60mph (0–96kph) time of around 13 seconds,

■ ABOVE *Extremely compact, the Fiat X1/9 brought the delights of mid-engine motoring to a wide public. Previously the layout had been the almost exclusive province of expensive exotics.*

FIAT X1/9 (1972–89)	
Engine	4-cylinder
Capacity	1290–1499cc
Power	75–85bhp
Transmission	4/5-speed manual
Top speed	100–110mph (161–177kph)
No. built	180,000

■ LEFT *Pop-up headlamps were a distinctive feature. This is a later-model X1/9 produced by the coachbuilder Bertone (which originally designed the car).*

■ FAR LEFT *Removing the standard targa roof panel produced a virtual convertible - great for sunny days, but practical as well.*

■ LEFT *If you thought, because the engine was in the middle, that you had luggage space in the front, you had to think again, as this picture shows.*

■ RIGHT *Despite its small-capacity engine, the X1/9 was a creditable performer for its day. 100mph (161kph) was available in all versions.*

but this was frankly a waste of its potential grip and razor-sharp handling. Even so, novices and seasoned drivers alike took it to their hearts because it was so easy to drive. The steering was light, precise and full of feel, and the balance of the car was neutral.

Even driven at its limit an X1/9 never snapped, but telegraphed its warnings miles ahead of an impending loss of adhesion. As a bonus, strut suspension gave a relatively comfortable, civilized ride. Fiat boss Agnelli even abandoned his limo so he could drive himself to work every day in an X1/9.

Extra performance was achieved in 1978 by using the 1500cc engine from the Ritmo/Strada hatchback. The revvy 1.5 unit would whistle round to nearly 7000rpm and turn in 30mpg economy. A good 1500 would touch 110mph (177kph), break 60mph (96kph) in

under 10 seconds and cruise at 100mph (161kph), but by then many ordinary high-performance hatchbacks could out-run it. You got five speeds with the 1500, but big impact bumpers had by then spoiled the once-crisp looks.

In 1982, production was taken over by Bertone, which continued to manufacture and market the car as the Bertone X1/9 until its demise in 1989. Late cars had desirable touches like leather seats, alloy wheels and electric windows. By then the car was notorious for appalling corrosion, and many of the early examples have long since disappeared from the road.

It wasn't until the mid-80s that it had a serious competitor in the shape of Toyota's MR2. There is no doubt that the little Fiat is the father of today's popular mid-engined sportscars. Fiat did not produce its own spiritual successor until the front-wheel-drive Barchetta of 1995.

■ RIGHT *Beautifully balanced handling was the main attraction of X1/9 ownership. The chassis was much more communicative than that of almost any other car of its price.*

■ FAR LEFT *A strict two-seater, the X1/9's cabin was cosy rather than spacious. The architecture was distinctly Italian.*

■ LEFT *The X1/9 left production in 1989 with no mid-engined successor. The plain fact was that developments in the front-engined layout had made it a more feasible proposition.*

FIAT

■ FIAT BARCHETTA

Barchetta is an Italian word meaning "little boat", and has come to describe a whole class of open-topped Italian sportscars. Fiat's version was undoubtedly one of the high points of the genre and applied Italian flair to the challenge laid down by the Mazda MX-5.

In style, the Barchetta was both retrospective and modern. The door handles, which popped out of the bodywork at the press of a button, harked back to a classic era, but purposely curvaceous body accent line and aerodynamic accoutrements

■ LEFT *Barchetta means "little boat" in Italian – a surprisingly fitting description for this diminutive sportscar, which boasted so much design flair.*

■ LEFT *Sportscar drivers felt immediately at home in the cockpit, which was relatively sparsely equipped but suitably angled towards the enthusiast's needs.*

■ ABOVE *On the road the Barchetta was a delight, combining zippy acceleration with tenacious cornering, light steering and a free-revving engine.*

FIAT BARCHETTA (1995–)

Engine	4-cylinder
Capacity	1747cc
Power	130bhp @ 6300rpm
Transmission	5-speed
Top speed	124mph (200kph)
No. built	Still in production

■ BELOW *The truncated tail with its oblong lamps contrasted with the long nose. The "humped" profile was emphasized by body side accents.*

reminded the casual onlooker that this was a contemporary sportscar.

It may have been based on the floorpan of the humble front-wheel-drive Fiat Punto, but the Barchetta packed a strong punch under its bonnet in the form of a new 1.75-litre fuel-injected 16V twin-cam engine. As the whole car weighed only just over one tonne (ton), performance was enjoyable and the engine would happily spin away up to 7000rpm. That spirited pace was matched by grippy cornering ability and super-sharp steering.

Inside there was a minor feast of detail, from the angled centre console and the smoothly sculpted doors to the intriguing eyeball vents. There might not have been much room for luggage, but this was a sportscar so that was to be expected.

Good value was another Barchetta strong point, and it sold particularly well in Italy. British customers had to make do with left-hand drive but even so were appreciative of the diminutive Fiat sportscar. After all, the Barchetta had all the makings of a genuine classic.

■ RIGHT *Bold slashes in the body sides, bisected door mirrors, a clamshell bonnet and a strongly wedged profile – this could only be Pininfarina's extraordinary design for the Fiat Coupé.*

■ FIAT COUPÉ

Pininfarina was extremely adventurous with its brief to design a new coupé for Fiat, which arrived in 1993. No one could ever mistake the Coupé for anything else, and even if its appeal was not universal, it had all the character you could ever wish for.

From the bold rising slashes in the flanks to the elegantly curved roof, and from the curious "double bubble" headlamp covers to the evocative circular tail lamps, the Coupé made a very strong statement.

Although in feel it seemed like a miniature Ferrari or Maserati, the new Coupé was actually based on the platform of the ageing Fiat Tipo. Considering this basis, Fiat engineers worked miracles to create such a fine-handling sports coupé as this. Limited slip differential kept the front wheels

from spinning when the accelerator was pressed to the floor, while tyre grip remained superb even at very high cornering forces.

At first, there was a choice of two 2.0-litre engines: a 142bhp 16V unit or a 195bhp Turbo. Both were quick but the Turbo was exceptional, having a 0–60mph (0–96kph) time of just over seven seconds. In 1995, the engine range was renewed, starting with the 131bhp Barchetta 1.8 and ending up with a pair of brand-new five-cylinder 2.0 units; the most powerful had a

turbocharger and no less than 220bhp – and was almost indecently quick.

Accommodation was surprisingly spacious for four people, although that meant boot (trunk) space was rather restricted. The adventurous themes of the bodywork were extended into the cabin, such as an effective swage of painted metal running right across the dashboard and doors.

■ BELOW *Few cars in any class handled as well as the Fiat Coupé, which boasted fine grip, sharp responses and entertaining handling for the driver.*

■ RIGHT *With its bold body-coloured finish through the middle of the dash, the Coupé felt very special. The driving position was excellent.*

FIAT COUPÉ (1993–)	
Engine	4/5-cylinder
Capacity	1747–1998cc
Power	131–220bhp
Transmission	5-speed
Top speed	127–155mph (204–249kph)
No. built	Still in production

■ RIGHT *From the rear, the styling was every bit as adventurous as from other angles. The circular rear lights recalled Farina designs for countless Ferraris.*

FORD

■ LEFT *Further modifications were incorporated for rallying homologation on this RS500 edition, including an extra 20bhp and an even bigger whale-tail spoiler.*

■ FORD SIERRA RS COSWORTH

The "Cossie" Sierra has passed into the annals of motoring history as the car that brought rally-style levels of power and grip to a broad public. Its phenomenal performance became a legend, all the more so because it was such exceptional value.

When, in 1986, Cosworth installed its new two-litre twin overhead-camshaft turbo engine into the Sierra bodyshell,

FORD SIERRA RS COSWORTH (1986–92)	
Engine	4-cylinder
Capacity	1993cc
Power	204–224bhp
Transmission	5-speed manual
Top speed	143–149mph (230–240kph)
No. built	26,771

■ ABOVE *Piloting the powerful RS500 was a very special experience, all the more so because a mere 500 examples were built in total.*

■ LEFT *The true "popular" Cosworth was the four-door Sapphire, built from 1988. A modest body kit package and sober clothing belied the car's tremendous ability.*

the inherently fine handling of Ford's rear-wheel-drive hatchback was matched by the power to exploit it. Its 204bhp was generous to say the least and the performance figures proved it: a top speed of 145mph (233kph) and 0–60mph (0–96kph) in 6.2 seconds. What was more, the engine could be easily tuned to stratospheric heights.

Ford's humble sales-rep special could now out-perform some Ferraris, yet it cost only £16,000 ($27,000) – about the same as a BMW 325i or Toyota Supra. The badge on the back – RS Cosworth – came to signify a performance icon.

In truth, the Cosworth may have looked superficially like a body-kitted Sierra but there was little resemblance under the skin. Ford's Special Vehicle Engineering department intended this to be a convincing Group A race and rally car (which it was), and decided to beef up the whole car. There was a close-ratio five-speed gearbox, limited slip differential, power steering, anti-lock braking, thick anti-roll bars, stiff suspension, wide alloy wheels and tyres, and huge disc brakes with four-piston calipers.

The bodywork incoporated no less than 92 modifications, from the widened wheel arches to the dramatic whale-tail spoiler. The aim was to increase

■ RIGHT *The massive rear aerofoil brought instant fame and recognition to the RS Cosworth. The intention was to increase downforce over the rear-end.*

■ LEFT *A genuine performance legend was created when Ford put its RS badge together with the Cosworth tuning company. It was scintillatingly quick, yet reasonably priced.*

downforce, which it did, but aerodynamics suffered, with the Cd falling to 0.34 and criticism coming from certain quarters about stability in cross-winds. Aesthetically, it was hardly subtle either. These drawbacks hardly mattered, however, to the drivers who revelled in the Cosworth's neck-snapping acceleration and finely balanced handling.

Because it was intended as a homologation special for racing, only 6021 Cosworth hatchbacks were made, plus an additonal 500 evolution RS500 models with 224bhp and an even larger rear spoiler. Their successor was the Sapphire Cosworth, a four-door model with much more restrained styling but all the driving ability of the earlier car. Added bonuses included greater practicality and more generous equipment levels.

The theme was extended in 1990 with the 4x4 version, developed to give the Sierra a better chance in rallying. The 4x4 gained an extra 16bhp, thanks to a new 16-valve cylinder head. That meant even more performance as well as sure-

footed handling, which left virtually every other car on the road for dead.

Having been in its lifetime the number one target for thieves and joy-riders in Britain, and hence almost impossible to insure, the "Cossie" has since assumed the mantle of a respected and affordable classic.

■ RIGHT *Able to reach 60mph (96 kph) from rest in a little over six seconds, this Ford, despite its humble origins, could outpace many so-called supercars.*

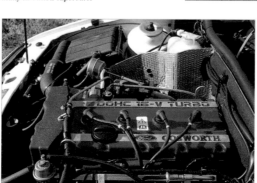

■ LEFT *Cosworth's 16-valve turbocharged engine produced 204bhp in its original form. Ford lost no opportunities in exploiting the Cosworth connection to the full.*

FORD

■ FORD RS200

In the 1980s, a new breed of supercar hit the streets. Manufacturers wanting to muscle in on the prestigious Group B rally scene were forced by the regulations to build a minimum of 200 cars for homologation purposes, which usually meant having to sell some as road-going cars. Many of these beasts, while brutally effective on forest roads, were hopelessly impractical if you had to drive anywhere on public roads.

Ford's Group B effort, the RS200, was certainly effective, but in road form it was also one of the most practical and comfortable of all, having such luxuries as a fully-trimmed cockpit and even provision for a radio. In racing terms, the RS200 never achieved its full potential because, after just one season (1986), the sport's governing body cancelled the Group B category. It was left to private entrants to pick up honours such as the European Rallycross Championship.

The RS200 was conceived as early as 1983 as a bespoke (dedicated) rally machine. Ghia styled the monocoque bodyshell, which was made of glassfibre and Kevlar over an aluminium honeycomb floor with steel front- and rear-box sections. It looked a good deal prettier than any other Group B car around. It was short and stubby yet had an undeniable presence, mainly thanks to its large tail spoiler and roof-mounted spoiler/air dam. The windscreen derived from the standard production Ford Sierra.

Cosworth provided the engine, a turbocharged, slightly enlarged BDT development of the BDA unit fitted to the Escort RS1700T. It developed 250bhp in road-going form and could be tuned as high as 450bhp – or even higher – for competition use.

The four-wheel-drive transmission was unusual in that the magnesium-

■ ABOVE *To make the most of the mid-engined layout, there was an unusual four-wheel-drive system developed by FF.*

■ LEFT *The RS200 arrived too late to have much impact on the doomed Group B rally scene, but it was a devastatingly effective rally machine.*

FORD RS200 (1984–86)	
Engine	4-cylinder
Capacity	1803cc
Power	250bhp
Transmission	5-speed
Top speed	140mph (225kph)
No. built	200

■ OPPOSITE *Ford's modestly-named RS200 was a full-blown bespoke (dedicated) rally car also sold for road use. Ghia styled the bodywork and Ford's rally department did the rest.*

■ RIGHT *The rally impetus is obvious in this picture of the hinging front and rear ends, the idea being to allow instant easy access to all the mechanical components.*

cased Hewland transaxle was mounted well away from the engine, immediately behind the front differential and effectively between the passengers' legs. This was, incidentally, Ford's first-ever four-wheel-drive road car

Because of the car's light weight (just 2315lb (1050kg)), it performed superbly. It could reach 60mph (96kph) in only six seconds, and top speed was quoted as 140mph (225kph), limited by a disappointing Cd figure of 0.40.

The RS200 was launched at the 1984 Turin Motor Show, but preproduction delays meant that the car did not get its homologation papers until early 1986, by which time the required 200 units had already been built. The demise of Group B meant RS200 production would never resume, although much development was later given to it to keep it competitive in racing well into the 1990s.

■ LEFT *Considering it was a rally car, the cockpit was surprisingly civilized, with its proper trimming, leather steering wheel and provision for a hi-fi system.*

■ LEFT *The mid-mounted engine was developed by Cosworth. Its capacity was only 1.8 litres, but its highly developed innards and turbocharging took standard power to 250bhp.*

■ ABOVE *The RS200 was effectively rendered obsolete by the demise of the Group B rally class, adjudged to be too fast and dangerous.*

HONDA

■ HONDA NSX

With all its reputation for mastery in engine and suspension technology, culminating in a successful Formula 1 racing programme, it is perhaps surprising that Honda did not attempt to produce a supercar before the NSX. When it did give the go ahead for this risky project, the end result was typically clean, business-like and incredibly effective: in essence, the NSX was the most user-friendly of an inherently impractical breed.

Here was a car that bristled with exciting yet pertinent features. Honda recognized the need for light weight, so specified an all-aluminium monocoque body and forged alloy suspension components, which were tested by racer Ayrton Senna. The abilities of the NSX can be judged by the fact that Senna owned several over the years, as did McLaren F1 engineer Gordon Murray.

It was simply the best supercar to drive and own, equally capable of idling around town as doing an impression of a Le Mans racer.

The 3.0-litre engine, which was mounted centrally, was a tour de force: four camshafts, 24 valves, variable valve

■ LEFT *In America the NSX was marketed under the Acura brand name. Elsewhere it was sold alongside humble Civics as a Honda.*

■ BELOW *Later versions of the NSX were faster, lighter and more powerful, and came with the option of a removable targa top.*

■ LEFT *Honda showed the prototype of its new NSX sportscar in 1989, and the world was prepared to make the acquaintance of one of the finest cars ever made.*

HONDA NSX (1990–)	
Engine	V-six-cylinder
Capacity	2977–3179cc
Power	270–294bhp
Transmission	5/6-speed manual, 4-speed automatic
Top speed	161–171mph (259–275kph)
No. built	Still in production

■ OPPOSITE *The NSX was designed to compete with Europe's best, such as Porsche and Ferrari. In absolute terms it was easily their equal, perhaps only lacking an indefinable excitement factor.*

■ LEFT *In typical Honda fashion, the NSX's lines were simple and unadorned. This was a devastatingly efficient machine in all respects.*

■ ABOVE *In motion, the 3.2-litre engine had a sound and a performance that denoted engineering purity. Road testers were struck by the sheer ability and range of its dynamics.*

timing and induction, titanium connecting rods, separate coils for each spark plug and an ability to rev to 8300rpm. Its power delivery was smooth, the throttle response was electric, and the noise it emitted ranged from a sweet purr to the scream of a thoroughbred racer. In short, the NSX engine was one of the all-time great power plants.

Its 270bhp was hugely impressive for a 3.0-litre engine. Even though by supercar standards its acceleration was not class-beating, 0–60mph (0–96kph) in 5.8 seconds could hardly be described as sluggish.

In handling terms, the NSX was both forgiving and communicative, aided by superb traction control and accurate steering. This was one of the true masters of the art of cornering.

The NSX was the most expensive car Japan had ever made, but its price still undercut rivals like the Ferrari 348. With almost no faults, it was unquestionably the most mature exponent of the supercar breed.

Later years saw it improve still further, and in 1997 it got the biggest revamp of its life, with a bigger 3.2-litre engine, six-speed gearbox, variable-weight power steering and bigger brakes. It remains one of the most respected cars in the world.

OTHER MAKES

■ HOLDEN

Holden is the Australian outpost of the global General Motors empire. Occasionally it produced or imported European and American GM products (and even badged many models produced by Japanese companies), but more usually it developed cars specially suited to the Australian market. Its main model lines included the Monaro, Commodore, Torana and Statesman, which were great cruising machines halfway between European and American idioms.

■ HYUNDAI

The biggest car-maker in Korea has always been Hyundai, and its current size is all the more impressive considering it only began making cars in 1967, producing a version of the Ford Cortina. Its first all-new car was the 1975 Pony designed by Giugiaro. Gradually, its allegiance to Ford switched to Mitsubishi, and it made several licence-built models in Korea. Its position in the West grew yearly stronger with burgeoning exports of conventional but cheap family cars.

■ INNOCENTI

Innocenti began life as the holder of licences to make BMC products in Italy, and it produced the Austin A40, Mini, 1100 and Allegro. In 1976, ownership passed from British Leyland to De Tomaso, which produced over 200,000 Bertone-styled small cars based on the Mini platform. Subsequently, it turned to Daihatsu for its engines. Fiat acquired the marque in the 1980s and kept the name for imported versions of the Fiat Uno, Yugo and Daihatsu Hijet. The marque survived until 1997.

■ ISUZU

In Britain, the Japanese Isuzu name is best known for its four-wheel-drive vehicles, and in America it is remembered for the Gemini (a version of the Opel Kadett world car). Isuzu is basically General Motors' foothold in Japan, but has also made some interesting models. The Bertone-styled 117 coupé of 1968–81 was a design classic, and its 1980s Giugiaro-designed Piazza coupé Impulse was a best-seller. More recently Isuzu has concentrated on licence-built Hondas and sport-utility vehicles.

JAGUAR

■ JAGUAR XJS

Jaguar had charmed the world with its glorious E-Type in 1961, but by 1975 this was looking decidedly outdated and needed a successor. That car was the XJS, a car which had all the ingredients in place to make it perhaps the greatest car in the world: a fabulous V-twelve engine, world-beating suspension and all the prestige of the Jaguar badge.

Somehow the XJS lost the magic that made the E-Type so great. The styling rubbed everyone up the wrong way: traditionalists bemoaned its slab flanks, trapezoidal headlamps and black rubber bumpers and asked what had happened

■ ABOVE *The styling attracted some controversy, particularly the treatment of the flying buttress rear pillars. The XJS was accused of a "design-by-committee" birth.*

to Jaguar's traditional grille, its chrome and its walnut veneer dashboard. Sportscar drivers questioned its curious flying buttress styling and cramped interior. The truth is that, unlike the E-Type, which was designed by one talented professional, the XJS was styled by committee and ended up being a compromise.

Jaguar chose to base the XJS on a shortened version of the XJ12 saloon (sedan) platform, so that it kept its drive train, suspension and brakes intact. The standard transmission was a Borg Warner three-speed automatic, and

■ ABOVE *The last XJS models benefited from a major revamp in terms of styling, interior treatment and new 4-litre six-cylinder and 6-litre V-twelve engines.*

■ RIGHT *Front-seat passengers were cosseted in impressive chairs, although those in the rear were severely limited for space.*

■ RIGHT *Every XJS model drove impressively. Some magazines were tempted to call it the best grand touring car available by virtue of its impeccable ride and excellent driving characteristics.*

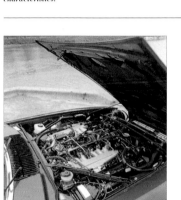

■ ABOVE *The fuel-injected V-twelve engine was a tight fit under the low bonnet-line (hood line), but the rewards were immeasurable since this was one of the finest engines produced.*

JAGUAR XJS (1975–96)	
Engine	6/V-twelve-cylinder
Capacity	3590–5994cc
Power	223–333bhp
Transmission	3/4-speed automatic 4/5-speed manual
Top speed	141–158mph (227–254kph)
No. built	112,000

although a manual gearbox was offered only 352 customers opted for it. Performance was superb for a grand touring four-seater, with a top speed of 150mph (241kph) and bustling acceleration.

The interior was based around the XJ saloon parts bin but featured a curious instrument binnacle with inset main dials and revolving minor gauges on the dash. There was plenty of space in the

front seats, but the rear pair was really suitable only for children.

The 5.3-litre V-twelve engine was given better fuel economy and more power in 1981 and re-christened XJS HE (High Efficiency). Now the XJS started to get some of the chrome and wood that had been missing. The range was expanded in 1983 by the addition of a six-cylinder 3.6-litre XJS and a brand-new Cabriolet model, which had rigid

targa roof panels and a folding rear section and was a strict two-seater. This drop-top model lasted until 1988, when it was replaced by a new top-of-the-range full Convertible V-twelve model with an electric folding roof. A TWR-developed 333bhp XJR-S version arrived at the same time.

For 1991, the XJS got a £50 million ($84 million) investment and a new lease of life. The bodyshell was heavily reworked, especially at the rear-end, and the interior was thoroughly revamped. Another major change was the adoption of the new AJ6 four-litre engine. Within three years this was uprated to AJ16 specification and got an extra 15bhp, while the venerable old V-twelve engine expanded to six litres.

The XJS survived until September 1996, making it the longest-lived Jaguar ever at over 21 years. One measure of its excellence is that its replacement, the XK8, was based on the XJS floorpan.

■ ABOVE *The first XJS models had no wood and little leather, but later examples redressed the imbalance.*

■ LEFT *The convertible XJS, which arrived quite late in the model's production career, was an extremely popular choice and highly rewarding to own.*

JAGUAR

■ JAGUAR XK8

After years of rumours about a true E-Type replacement called the F-Type, Jaguar finally presented its crucial new sportscar, the XK8, at the 1996 Geneva Motor Show.

Officially, this was the replacement for the XJS, but it had so much more appeal that it was really viewed as the spiritual successor to the E-Type. Its svelte lines were created at Jaguar's design head-quarters in Whitley, West Midlands, and it was engineered using the XJS floorpan as its starting-point. The XK8 delivered a distinct blend of style, luxury, craftsmanship and performance in a car that was uniquely British in flavour.

Central to the new design was the all-aluminium AJV-eight engine, the very first V-eight engine ever produced by Jaguar, after an investment of £200 million ($337 million). The 32-valve quad-cam engine delivered power, smoothness and refinement and had such advanced features as variable cam phasing, platinum-tipped spark plugs, split-block cooling and catalysts that began operating only 30 seconds after start-up. The ZF transmission was also new, Jaguar's first five-speed automatic. Other technical advances were electronic variable ratio power-steering, new

■ ABOVE *Jaguar rightly played on the heritage of its E-Type sportscar, for the XK8 was its spiritual successor. Unlike the XJS, it was a genuine sportscar, as well as a comfortable grand tourer.*

JAGUAR XK8 (1996–)	
Engine	V-eight-cylinder
Capacity	3996cc
Power	290 bhp
Transmission	5-speed auto
Top speed	154mph (248kph)
No. built	Still in production

■ LEFT *Underneath the bonnet of the latest sleek cat lay Jaguar's first-ever V-eight engine, the AJ-V8, which was a technical tour de force.*

■ ABOVE *Rich traditions of leather and wood were kept up, and the game was moved on by the installation of state-of-the-art high-tech electronics.*

■ LEFT *The fabulous XK8 was the successor to the long-running XJS and was a quantum leap beyond it, even though its floorpan was merely an XJS derivation.*

■ LEFT *The design of the XK8 was completed entirely in-house, and revived the glory days of Jaguar's founder William Lyons.*

■ BELOW *The XK8's striking similarity to the Aston Martin DB7 was not lost on many observers. The XK8 was, however, considerably cheaper to buy.*

computer-active double-wishbone front suspension, XJR-derived rear suspension and multiplexed (integrated) electronics.

The result of all this technology was a car which performed superbly. Indeed, it went as fast as the Aston Martin DB7 (a car designed by the same team), and many hailed the far cheaper XK8 as a better car all round. Refined yet explosively fast, smooth yet sporting in character, the XK8 was a brilliant grand tourer and sportscar.

Launched just after the coupé at the New York Motor Show was a convertible with an electric top, which raised in just 20 seconds. Unlike some competitors, the soft top stacked up behind the seats in order not to compromise boot (trunk) space. With the top raised the XK8 felt just as refined as the coupé. The cabin oozed classic-leather ambience and was available in two styles: fashionable art-style "Sport" and full "Classic" treatment with walnut trim and colour-coordinated carpets. All models had air-conditioning, electric seats and cruise control, while audiophiles could specify a Harman Kardon hi-fi.

The XK8 maintained Jaguar's reputation for best-in-class ride and handling. A good example of Jaguar's attention to detail was the fact that each aircraft-spec aluminium front-suspension cross-beam was X-ray inspected prior to installation.

■ LEFT *The addition of a convertible model boosted the XK8's appeal. The soft top could be raised electronically in only 20 seconds.*

■ BELOW *Jaguar's noble sports-roadster heritage stretches back to the SS100 of the 1930s, and the XK8 justifiably took its place alongside the greats.*

JAGUAR

■ JAGUAR XJ220

There are very few production cars that can claim to be have been born out of a spare-time project, but the Jaguar XJ220 is the most famous of all. Jaguar's chief engineer, Jim Randle, dreamt up the idea of creating the ultimate supercar one Christmas and fired up enough enthusiasm with colleagues to start a "Saturday club" to work on the project.

At first not even the Jaguar board knew about the secret tinkering going at its Engineering Department at Whitley in the West Midlands of Britain. When it did find out, the enthusiasm bubbled over, and the new XJ220 was wheeled out at the 1988 Birmingham Motor Show as an official Jaguar concept car. The prototype XJ220 was an immense beast, mainly because it had to be accommodated around TWR racing components and Jaguar's massive V-twelve engine mounted in a central position. Still, Keith Helfet's aluminium bodywork design was a sublime piece of sculpture.

■ LEFT *The V-six engine had twin turbochargers and racing-car-type materials and construction. Its output was a remarkable 500bhp.*

The response at the 1988 show was rapturous, and the affluence of the times persuaded Jaguar to embark on a production run. Because of production practicalities the design was substantially modified. It was decided that the V-twelve engine was too bulky and so a race-derived 3.5-litre V-six engine was installed instead. Its state-of-the-art specification included four camshafts, twin injectors, twin turbochargers, four valves per cylinder and dry sump lubrication, and it was capable of pumping out 500bhp.

JAGUAR XJ220 (1991–94)	
Engine	V-six-cylinder
Capacity	3498cc
Power	500bhp @ 6500rpm
Transmission	5-speed
Top speed	220mph (352kph)
No. built	350

■ LEFT *After it was presented as a prototype in 1988, the public clamour surrounding the fastest Jaguar ever made persuaded the company to enter production with the XJ220.*

■ OPPOSITE *The imposing authority of the XJ220 was confirmed by anyone who drove it. Here was a car which had phenomenal dynamic ability, helped by aircraft-inspired engineering.*

The smaller engine meant that overall length could be trimmed down by a sizeable 10in (25cm), but there was no escaping the massive girth of this sportscar: at 6ft 6in (nearly two metres) wide, this was the broadest British car ever made.

The specification sheet of the XJ220 read like a sportscar-driver's dream. Its bodywork was an aerospace type bonded-aluminium honeycomb with Group C racing inspired aerodynamics, the five-speed transaxle was mated to a racing AP clutch, there were centre-lock (knock-off) alloy wheels, massive brakes with four-piston calipers and racing-derived wishbone/inboard suspension.

Jaguar's performance claims were equally exciting. Its top speed of 220mph (352kph) and 0–60mph (0–96kph) time of 3.5 seconds made it easily the fastest road car on earth at the time. In-gear acceleration was

■ ABOVE *The best place to enjoy the full performance of the XJ220 – 220mph (352kph) – was undoubtedly a race-track,* for the immense girth and negligible visibility made it difficult to exploit its potential on real-world roads.*

absolutely brutal. To match that explosive power, the racing suspension made the XJ220 probably the best-handling supercar ever.

A joint Jaguar–TWR venture called JaguarSport set up a brand new production facility in Bloxham, Oxfordshire, to make a strictly limited run of 350 cars, each priced at £403,000 ($678,000). At first, the order book was over-subscribed by speculators but, when it became obvious that the market for supercars had collapsed, legal proceedings ensued as buyers tried to pull out – an ignominious end to an amazing story.

■ RIGHT *The impeccable detailing reflected the XJ220's hand-built nature and extraordinary price.*

■ LEFT *For all its exotic specification, the interior was a thoroughly comfortable place to be. There was room for luxury even at stratospheric speeds.*

■ ABOVE *In high-speed tests the XJ220 proved capable of speeds approaching 220mph (352kph), and of reaching 60mph (96kph) from rest in just 3.5 seconds.*

JEEP

■ LEFT *Where the legend started: the Second World War Willys Jeep was conceived in double-quick time, and it got on with its job. It inspired a whole dynasty of civilian jeeps.*

■ JEEP

The great American legend that is the Jeep has its origins in desperate times. In June 1940, the US Quartermaster Corps published requirements for a compact 4x4 quarter-ton truck. It asked potential contractors that a fully functioning prototype should be ready within one month. Of 135 firms polled to do this near-impossible job, only two took up the challenge: Willys–Overland

(which asked for an extra 45 days to prepare a car) and a small Detroit engineering firm called Bantam, which got the contract.

Production started at Ford, Willys and Bantam factories. The basic chassis was a box-section twin-rail frame with cross-members, fitted with low-carbon steel bodywork, ultra-simple for ease of manufacture. To enable Jeeps to be stacked on top of each other, the windscreen was removable.

Suspended by leaf springs (and dampers – shocks – only at the rear), the Jeep was powered by Willys's "Go-Devil" 2.2-litre four-cylinder unit with

aluminium pistons, producing only 49bhp but a massive 105lb ft (142Nm) of torque at just 2000rpm. Drivers had three gears to choose from, plus a two-speed transfer box and switchable freewheel for the front axle.

It was basic in the extreme, but the hastily conceived design was inherently right: no major changes were made despite the arduous tests of war use. Over 600,000 of these machines were churned out until the end of production in 1945, after which the French firm Hotchkiss made Jeeps into the 1960s.

After the war, Willys plugged on with the Jeep in civilian CJ-2A form, with the advertising line, "The sun never sets on

■ ABOVE *The whole jeep story can be traced through these cars, from the Second World War fighter through the CJ models at the rear, and up to date with the Wrangler editions of the 1980s and 1990s.*

■ RIGHT *This 1990 Wrangler Laredo proves the durability of the Jeep phenomenon. The famous hallmarks of square-cut wings, simple flat surfaces and grille all remain.*

■ LEFT *Modern Jeep Wranglers in their element, crossing the most inhospitable terrain. Jeeps gradually became more lifestyle vehicles than working cars.*

■ BELOW LEFT *A whole new strain of Jeeps was launched with the Cherokee, a multi-purpose 4x4 four-door. This is one of the compact modern versions, dating from 1984.*

■ BELOW RIGHT *Although this is merely a concept exercise called the Jeep Freedom, it shows there is a spiritual connection between the Cherokee and original-type Jeeps.*

the Willys-built Jeep". Farmers loved them, and Jeeps provided cheap, practical transportation in austere times.

The 1946 Station Wagon was America's first steel-bodied estate. The body was recognizably Jeep, but it was on a longer wheelbase, had a six-cylinder engine option and only two-wheel drive. It had non-structural wood applied to its sides and split rear doors. Even more "civvy" was the Brooks

Stevens-styled Jeepster with its bright colour schemes, whitewall tyres, luxurious fittings and detachable hood. The Jeepster name was revived briefly in 1967.

The Jeep CJ evolved slowly, the CJ5 and long-wheelbase CJ6 versions lasting from 1952 into the 1970s, by which time AMC had become the parent company. An important variant was the 1972 CJ5 Renegade, a sporty Jeep with a V-eight

engine, which pointed the way ahead in terms of style development.

Gradually, the range expanded to include the Commando pickup, the four-door Wagoneer and, from 1974, Cherokee sport-utilities. While the CJ soldiered on around the world, in America the Cherokee and larger Grand Cherokee assumed greater significance, as well as "retro" reworkings of the original idea, sold under the name Wrangler.

JEEP WRANGLER (1986–)	
Engine	4/6-cylinder
Capacity	2464–4235cc
Power	112–184bhp
Transmission	5-speed manual 3/4-speed auto
Top speed	84–108mph (130–174kph)
No. built	Still in production

■ RIGHT *Largest of the jeep family is the Grand Cherokee with its large-capacity V-eight engine and very comfortable interior.*

LAMBORGHINI

■ LAMBORGHINI COUNTACH

To top the amazing mid-engined Miura, unquestionably the most exotic car of the 1960s, Lamborghini had to come up with something decisively more dramatic. In that at least the amazing Countach succeeded superbly.

The original bright-yellow Bertone-styled prototype of 1971 was dramatic yet remarkably pure and unadorned compared with the more familiar models of the late 1970s and 80s. Where the Miura had been sensual and muscular, the Countach was futuristic, razor-edged,

■ RIGHT *Banana-shaped leather seats looked more enticing than they really were. Luxury was not squandered in the Countach cabin.*

wedgey, breathing aggression from every pore. Wild as it looked, the Countach was a much better developed car than the flawed Miura, even though it was no easier to live with, owing to the problems with the show-off lift-up doors.

It was a sensation to drive, of course: as well as being more forgiving in its handling – the gearbox was now mounted in-line, ahead of the engine between the seats – it was even faster than the Miura: good for 186mph (299kph), claimed Lamborghini, if you could find a stretch of road long enough. Most road testers managed about 160mph (257kph).

The word *"countach"* is a Piedmontese expletive meaning wow – or something stronger depending on how it was pronounced. The first Countach went to

■ ABOVE *Opening the doors was as dramatic an experience as seeing the car for the first time. This is an LP500 model from 1982.*

■ LEFT *The trapezoidal tail lamps were an unmistakable Countach hallmark, punctuating one of the longest rear decks of any production car.*

LAMBORGHINI COUNTACH (1974–91)	
Engine	V-twelve-cylinder
Capacity	3929–5167cc
Power	375–455bhp
Transmission	5-speed manual
Top speed	186–200mph (299–322kph)
No. built	609

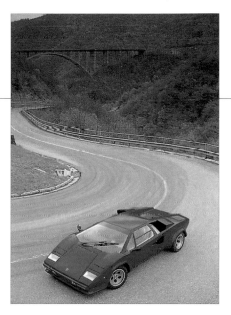

■ RIGHT *Fast, winding roads were the Countach's element, where it was almost indecently fast. Owners were always attracted as much by its brash character as by its raw ability.*

its owner in 1974 amid a blaze of publicity. However, the clean lines of the original became progressively more tasteless as the years went by, especially once the LP500 five-litre model appeared in 1982: its spoilers did nothing for stability, while big ugly wheel-arches housed improbably fat tyres, matched by even bigger NACA ducts to get air into the enlarged engine.

It also became apparent that build quality was merely adequate and the car began to put on as much flab as muscle. Yet its unremittingly powerful character overcame such quibbles and kept the

■ BELOW *Lamborghini's raging bull emblem was sustained by the success of the long-running Countach.*

■ ABOVE *The very last Countach QV models got yet another restyle and a four-valves-per-cylinder head. The model was retired finally in 1991.*

■ LEFT *The powerhouse in the middle of the Countach was a fabulously expressive V-twelve engine, claimed to return 200mph (322kph) performance.*

troubled Lamborghini – long since out of its founder's control – afloat through the dark abyss of the 70s and 80s when lesser models like the Urraco and Jalpa failed to find buyers. Having said that, the Countach never enjoyed the commercial success of Ferrari's much less radical Boxer and Testarossa.

The ultimate QV model – indicating Quattro Valvole (or four valves per cylinder) – bowed out in 1991. By then, its top speed was quoted as 200mph (322kph). In later years, the Countach had become a kind of parody of itself – a car for anybody with too much money and not enough taste – but at least it was recognizable.

■ ABOVE *No one was in any doubt that the Countach was a very quick machine, but in the latter half of its life Lamborghini felt* *obliged to add aerodynamic aids such as giant rear spoilers. In practice they had little effect beyond visual stimulation.*

LAMBORGHINI

■ LAMBORGHINI LM002

When you look at the back catalogue of Lamborghini cars, you will find only high-performance supercars: names like Miura, Countach, Espada, Diablo. There is one name that sticks out in this sleek, knee-high company: what on earth is an LM?

To realize why Lamborghini produced the equivalent of Mad Max, you have to understand why most European farmers are also familiar with the Lamborghini name: its other main business is making agricultural tractors. The LM002 was the perfect, if audacious, synthesis of these two sides of Lamborghini's business – a four-wheel-drive monster with a V-twelve Countach engine!

Its story actually begins with a request to produce a military vehicle for the US, in conjunction with Chrysler. This resulted in the Cheetah of 1977, a massive doorless all-terrain buggy with a mid-mounted Chrysler V-eight engine.

■ ABOVE *Dauntingly large wheels and tyres were specially designed to withstand large, sharp rocks.*

■ ABOVE *Straddling an immense central tunnel, four passengers could be seated in air-conditioned, leather-lined comfort. There was space for four or more on the pick-up rear-bed.*

■ ABOVE *The V-twelve engine from the Countach was stuffed under the bonnet to make a thundering beast in every sense. It had to be mounted rather high up.*

The tail-heavy weight distribution under which this layout suffered led the American government elsewhere (the US-built Hummvee, or Hummer, got the deal in the end).

Lamborghini pressed ahead with its own interpretation of the ultimate off-roader. Its production LM002 was shown for the first time in autumn 1985 with a Lamborghini Countach V-twelve engine up front. Everything about it was bigger and better than any other car.

The LM was immense. At over 16ft (495cm) long, it was about the same length as a Jaguar XJ, and it was over 6ft 6in (200cm) wide, 73in (185cm) high and weighed nearly 3 tonnes (2.95 tons). It could seat four people inside, two on each side of the largest central tunnel ever seen in a car, and four-to-six more passengers could perch in the pick-up rear. The enormous 345 x 17 tyres were specially made by Pirelli.

That giant Countach engine meant the LM was the fastest off-roader in the world: it could lug the LM up to a top speed of 126mph (201kph), while its 0–60mph (0–96kph) time of 8.5 seconds

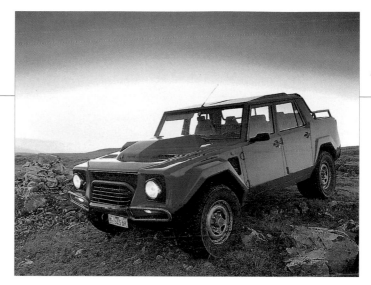

■ RIGHT *The audacity which produced the LM002 can only be gawped at. This leviathan was conceived as an all-terrain army vehicle but found favour with anyone with enough money and a desperate need to cross deserts at terminal velocities.*

could embarrass quite a few sportscars. The trade-off was fuel consumption in the region of 7mpg (11.2kpg) – you really needed the 70-gallon (318 litre) fuel tank. Off-road ability was deeply impressive thanks to the all-independent suspension and massive ground clearance.

If you were used to the utility treatment in your off-roader, the LM packed a few surprises. Here was a tough brute with all the fancy trimmings of a limousine: leather upholstery, air-conditioning, lots of electric gadgets, a wood dashboard and deep-pile carpeting.

The LM's natural habitat was the Middle East, where the military and the oil barons lapped it up, and that's just as well because the LM cost even more than the Countach and you really needed your own oil well to run one.

■ LEFT *The world's biggest bonnet (hood) bulges were required to clear the most powerful engine ever fitted to a standard 4x4 vehicle.*

LAMBORGHINI LM002 (1985–93)	
Engine	V-twelve-cylinder
Capacity	5167cc
Power	450bhp @ 6800rpm
Transmission	5-speed, drive to all four wheels
Top speed	126mph (203kph)
No. built	n/a

■ LEFT *On the road the LM002 turned into a GTI, capable of 126mph (203kph) and 0–60mph (0–96kph) in 8.5 seconds. The pay-off was the greediest fuel consumption figures ever recorded for a production car.*

LAMBORGHINI

■ OPPOSITE *A fiendish coven of Diablos: SV, racing SV-R, Roadster, standard two-wheel-drive and VT four-wheel-drive models.*

■ LAMBORGHINI DIABLO

"Diablo" means devil in Spanish, a curious choice for the Italian successor to the legendary Countach. The Diablo was the first fruit of Lamborghini's brief spell under Chrysler's wing, and cost £50 million ($84 million) to develop.

Following the Countach was never going to be easy, but the Diablo succeeded. Above all it looked absolutely startling thanks to the gifted penwork of Marcello Gandini. The dramatic scissor-type doors were retained for the new car and incorporated a deeply swooping waistline. The tail seemed to stretch back for ever, its long centre cut-out full of louvres, its air dams looking purposeful, its profile widening all the way. The nose could hardly have been lower or more stubbed. Construction was of aluminium and composite-plastic body panels over a chassis reinforced with carbonfibre.

Mechanically, the Diablo looked back to the Countach for its inspiration. Its V-twelve engine was a development of the Countach's, expanded, catalyzed and given sequential fuel injection. The result was 492bhp and 428ft

■ ABOVE *Even faster than the Countach it replaced, the Diablo – or "devil" – was a true giant of the supercar world.*

LAMBORGHINI DIABLO (1990–)	
Engine	V-twelve-cylinder
Capacity	5729cc
Power	492–525bhp
Transmission	5-speed
Top speed	186–210mph (299–338kph)
No. built	Still in production

(1404cm) of torque, plus one of the most fulfilling soundtracks of any engine. There was also a new five-speed gearbox geared so that 100mph (161kph) could be reached in second gear.

Lamborghini claimed that the Diablo's top speed of 202mph (325kph) could beat arch-rival Ferrari's F40. It was certainly very quick, as tests of the even more powerful, lightweight limited-edition 525bhp SE30 would show: 0–60mph (0–96kph) in 4.2 seconds was exceptionally rapid. Only its bulk and the heaviness of its steering knocked the edge off this good machine.

■ LEFT *An improbably long tail housed the engine, while the scissor-type doors were a continuation of the theme first seen in the Countach.*

■ ABOVE *The exceptionally neat-looking V-twelve engine developed no less than 492bhp in its original – and least powerful – guise.*

■ ABOVE *On its way to a 202mph (325 kph) top speed the Diablo would leave behind it a plume of smoke from the quad-exit exhausts – and a terrifying noise.*

■ ABOVE *In Lamborghini's vocabulary, SV meant Sport Veloce. In other words, it signified light weight, massive (510bhp) power and special gearing tuned for maximum acceleration.*

■ LEFT *A Ferrari-style exposed gear-lever gate fronts an impressive array of standard controls. The air-conditioning system was complex enough to fill the front compartment.*

Most of the Countach weaknesses – cramped interior, poor visibility, difficult access – were resolved in the Diablo. Luggage space was still at a premium, but the cabin looked and felt classy, boasted a great driving position and featured a control to adjust the suspension settings from the driver's seat. Lamborghini was confident that it could sell 500 cars a year, far more than the Countach had ever achieved.

New for 1991 was the VT (Viscous Transmission) model with full four-wheel drive, although the front wheels only ever got a maximum of 29 per cent of the overall power, and then only after the rear end began to lose traction. Four-wheel drive made the already fine handling even more assured, and the standard adoption of power steering made life behind the wheel much easier, although the penalty was the higher overall weight of the car.

Other variations followed in 1996. The Roadster was just what it said it was: a Diablo with a removable roof, intended to do battle with the similarly configured Ferrari F50. The SV (for Sport Veloce) was the most focused of all the Diablos: a 510bhp engine, lighter weight, lower gearing and even more startling acceleration (although the top speed dropped to "only" 186mph (299kph) owing to the new gearing). There was little doubt that this was the best of the exclusive Diablo family.

■ LEFT *The Roadster version had a hardtop which could be removed completely or pushed back and fixed above the engine bay.*

LANCIA

■ LANCIA GAMMA

When Fiat took control of Lancia and its huge debts in 1969, many pundits guessed that there would be no more true Lancias – technically advanced cars with sporting character. They were wrong. The Pininfarina-styled Gamma saloon (sedan) and coupé announced at Geneva in 1976 boasted all the idiosyncrasies associated with Lancia.

■ LEFT *The 1976 Gamma was Lancia's stab at the executive car market. The big four-door model was always a rare sight, as it seemed to be bought almost exclusively by Italian embassies.*

■ ABOVE *For an interior conceived in the mid-1970s, this was unusually attractive and stylish.*

■ ABOVE *It was perhaps a strange choice to fit a four-cylinder engine in a luxury car, one of the biggest "fours" then in production.*

Not the least of these quirks was the adoption of a big 2.5-litre flat-four engine in an executive class more used to six cylinders at the very least. Although the engine was torquey and smooth at high revs, it proved a difficult choice for buyers to accept, not only

because it was rather throbby and unrefined at tick-over but because it rapidly acquired a reputation for serious reliability problems: overheating was common, and the cam belt could strip its teeth if the steering was put on full lock from cold.

It was a shame that the Gamma was so underdeveloped because it was a great driving machine, with superb balance and the best power steering around. The saloon was handsome in its own way, but the coupé was a classic of elegant, perfectly proportioned styling.

Series 2 models gained fuel injection, a four-speed auto option and other detail modifications to make the engine more reliable, but it all came too late and in 1984 Gamma production ended. Had the model survived it would probably have been given effective 16-valve technology and there were even turbocharged 180bhp "Federalized" Gammas running as prototypes.

Pininfarina built a Spider version of the coupé in 1978, then a four-door, three-box Scala in 1980, and finally the Olgiata of 1982, a handsome estate (station wagon) version, but sadly all three remained prototypes.

■ LEFT *Very communicative steering and balanced handling made the Gamma a real driver's car. Performance was respectable.*

LANCIA GAMMA (1977–84)	
Engine	4-cylinder
Capacity	2500cc
Power	140bhp
Transmission	5-speed manual 4-speed auto
Top speed	120mph (193kph)
No. built	22,085

■ LANCIA MONTECARLO

This interesting mid-engined sportscar began life in the Fiat empire as a future sister model for the little X1/9. Indeed, the project was referred to under the name X1/20, but a shuffle of priorities then switched the new model under Lancia's wing.

The Montecarlo was launched at the 1975 Geneva Motor Show in both fixed coupé and targa-topped "Spider" versions. Its clean lines, featuring prominent black bumpers, a forward-thrusting snout and rear flying buttresses, created a stir with fans.

Much of the car was plundered from the parts bin of the Lancia Beta range,

■ ABOVE *The first-series Montecarlo was criticized for its braking performance and wet-weather roadholding, and was actually withdrawn from production for two years.*

■ ABOVE *The Montecarlo brochure celebrated Lancia's racing achievements with its mid-engined sportscar.*

■ LEFT *Pininfarina created the pretty shape of the Montecarlo around mid-engine ideals. Note the rear flying buttresses.*

■ ABOVE *The cockpit was strictly for two passengers, but boasted Italian design flair and a removable targa roof panel.*

LANCIA MONTECARLO (1978–84)	
Engine	4-cylinder
Capacity	1995cc
Power	120bhp
Transmission	5-speed
Top speed	118mph (190kph)
No. built	7595

■ RIGHT *Lancia's Montecarlo was the up-market sister of the Fiat X1/9, larger and more powerful, but no less attractive and very good value.*

including its 2.0-litre engine and many detail items. That kept costs down, and enabled Lancia to sell a car that many likened to a miniature Ferrari for a bargain price.

The story was not all roses, however. The engine was not really powerful enough for a true sportscar, the roadholding was positively dangerous in wet conditions, and severe front-wheel lock-up under braking forced Lancia to suspend production in 1978 pending an 18-month-long return to the proverbial drawing board.

When the Montecarlo reappeared in 1980, Lancia had addressed the problems: the front brake problem was cured by removing the servo assistance and the tail-happy nature was tamed by revised suspension. Also new were the grille, bigger wheels and a six-year anti-corrosion warranty.

In America, the Montecarlo was sold as the Scorpion with a dreadfully underpowered 80bhp 1.8-litre engine. When production ended in 1984 there was no direct replacement, and this was effectively the last real Lancia sportscar.

LANCIA

LANCIA DELTA INTEGRALE

In Italian, "*Integrale*" means full, complete, whole, and that fittingly describes the abilities of Lancia's impressive Delta Integrale. Although it was conceived as a car to homologate for rallying, it was quickly recognized as one of the all-time great road cars.

Lancia was a consistently strong rallying contender – one has only to remember the Stratos and 037 – and it had built the mid-engined four-wheel-drive Delta S4 Group 4 car in 1984. However, after such Group B monsters were banned following major crashes and deaths (prompting the nickname "Killer B's"), all attention switched to the milder Group A category for 1987.

Lancia produced the Delta HF 4x4 all-wheel-drive car as a prelude to the full Integrale model, which was launched in October 1987, with its distinctive wide wheel-arches and fat tyres. The Integrale promptly swept the board in rallying events, taking 14

■ LEFT *The magical "HF Integrale" badge came to mean everything that was desirable in performance-car terms.*

■ ABOVE *Across country there was hardly a car that could match the Integrale's pace and roadholding.*

LANCIA DELTA INTEGRALE (1988–94)	
Engine	4-cylinder
Capacity	1995cc
Power	185–215bhp
Transmission	5-speed manual
Top speed	130–137mph (209–220kph)
No. built	Approx 25,000

■ LEFT *It was across rough terrain that the Integrale shone. In World Championship rallies, it was dominant for many years.*

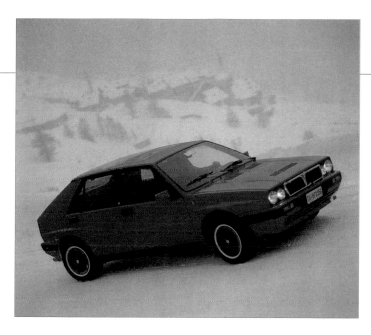

■ RIGHT *In adverse weather conditions, an Integrale was one of the best machines to pilot: safe yet also quick.*

World Championship rallies in 18 months and powering Miki Biasion to two world titles.

Road-car drivers quickly realized what a fabulous machine it was. The sophisticated four-wheel-drive system glued the car to the tarmac, while the 185bhp two-litre turbo engine sprinted the car across country faster than just about anything on the road. This was the fastest, safest point-to-point car in the world – and it was a practical five-door hatchback into the bargain. It felt special inside too: there were Recaro seats, electric front windows and unique instrumentation.

The Integrale just got better with age. In 1989, the old eight-valve cylinder head was upgraded to a new 16-valve head, which pushed power up to 200bhp. The main reason was to homologate the head for rallying, and it took only a few months to sell 5000 cars. The 16V cars won 13 World Championship rallies, and Kankkunen drove one to the 1991 title.

In 1991, a further evolution HF Integrale boasted even more power (210bhp – and later 215bhp – thanks to a larger exhaust), even wider wheel-arch flares to cover extended front and rear tracks, restyled grille, air intakes, bonnet, wings, bumpers and skirts, and a dramatic new adjustable tailgate spoiler. Officially, this edition was called just HF Integrale (no "Delta" in the name). It took until early 1992 to sell the requisite 5000 copies, and yet again Lancia took the 1992 Championship for Makes, in its last year as an official works team – not bad for a car that had its roots in the 1970s.

Today the Integrale has a hallowed status among keen drivers. Although it left production in 1994, examples are avidly sought after because there really is nothing like it still in production.

■ BELOW *Cornering at improbable speeds was the Integrale's true forte, and it could show its heels to just about everything else on the road.*

■ ABOVE *Lancia's Delta Integrale did not take long to make a huge impact on the motoring world. Its devastatingly effective brew of all-wheel drive and performance led to it becoming a legend in its own lifetime.*

LEXUS

■ LEXUS SC

In 1989, Toyota set out to beat Europe's finest marques at their own game. It wanted to steal a march on Mercedes-Benz, BMW and Jaguar by producing the world's best luxury saloon (sedan) – even though it had no experience in this market area. It invented a new brand, Lexus, sent its designers to California to discover what customers really wanted, and came up with the LS400 saloon, a car which signally succeeded in providing a genuine alternative to Europe's classic brands.

Lexus did not stop at the LS saloon, which was supremely competent but ultra-conservative in character. In 1991, it added a bit of spice into its new brand with a coupé version, known in the USA as the Lexus SC and in Japan as the

■ ABOVE *In export markets, the svelte Toyota-built coupé was badged as a Lexus SC. This is a top-of-the-range SC400 model.*

■ RIGHT *Overall the Lexus offered fine value, superlative build quality, attractive styling and crushing ability.*

■ LEFT *Highly sophisticated electronics dominated the engine bay of the SC. Several engines were built, from 2.5 litres to 4 litres.*

■ BELOW *Based on the successful Lexus LS400 four-door saloon (sedan), the coupé version added style and a sporting slant. Japanese versions were called Toyota Soarer.*

LEXUS SC (1991–)	
Engine	6-cylinder
Capacity	2491–3969cc
Power	225–280bhp
Transmission	5-speed manual 4-speed automatic
Top speed	146–155mph (235–250kph)
No. built	Still in production

■ BELOW *Satellite navigation was a novelty in 1991. In addition, all the air-conditioning functions were controlled from this LCD screen.*

■ RIGHT *The Toyota Soarer took off not only in Japan but also in America, where it stole sales from the prestige coupés of Mercedes-Benz and BMW.*

Toyota Soarer (it was never officially marketed in Europe).

The most striking aspect of the SC was the clean, restrained yet dramatic shape, created in Toyota's California studio. Although it was based on the floorpan of the Lexus saloon, the profile was fresh and boasted many beautiful touches, such as spotlamps shrouded by the subtlest of bulges running the whole length of the bonnet (hood).

In Japan, the catchphrase for the Soarer was "for mind cruising" – which conveyed the new model's primary objective: to transport its occupants over long distances in relaxation and comfort. It also happened to be sizzlingly quick.

The new SC range spanned three engine sizes, from a 225bhp 3.0-litre straight six up to the 4.0-litre V-eight used in the Lexus saloon; not sold in the US, the most powerful member of the family was the 2.5-litre Twin Turbo in-line-six engine, developing 20bhp more than the 4.0-litre V-eight, at 280bhp. The 4.0-litre engine scored 0–60mph (0–96kph) in 6.9 seconds with an automatic gearbox, while the five-speed manual Twin Turbo was nearer six seconds dead.

There was also a choice of three suspension systems. The first was conventional springing. The second was Piezo TEMS, an electronic air-suspension

■ LEFT *An all-digital dashboard was perhaps a little gimmicky but it fitted the high-tech nature of the Lexus perfectly.*

system, which obviated the need for conventional shock absorbers. Controlled by a microchip in the central electronic management computer, it adjusted each wheel's suspension according to the load on it at any given time. Top models got full Active Suspension.

Toyota's engineers went to great lengths to make driving the Soarer an

easy experience. Progressive power steering, which stiffened up as speed increased, limited slip differential and a powerful ABS system eradicated the worries of piloting such a potent machine. Seating was comfortable and the cabin was full of gadgets: satellite navigation, an all-electronic dash with touch-sensitive controls and a television.

■ RIGHT *With full active-ride suspension, the Lexus was a forgiving and accomplished cornerer. Its ride was also superior to that of almost any coupé in its class.*

LOTUS

■ LOTUS ESPRIT

Colin Chapman, the founder of Lotus, always said that he built the cars he wanted to own, which explained why, as he grew older, his designs matured into ever more sophisticated realms. By the early 1970s, the days of stark Lotus 7s sold in kit form were gone and a new era was dawning.

Chapman was extremely impressed by a mid-engined prototype, which Giorgetto Giugiaro had created for Lotus in 1972. This was the car that, with remarkably little modification, became the new Lotus Esprit, first shown in October 1975.

In construction, the Esprit was classically Lotus, having a steel-backbone chassis, all-independent suspension and a glassfibre body. As launched it had Lotus's brilliant 2.0-litre 16-valve four-cylinder engine mounted amidships. This not only

■ ABOVE *Clean lines, a mid-mounted engine and Lotus's fabled handling prowess made the Esprit a desirable, if flawed, sportscar.*

■ ABOVE *The interior architecture of the Esprit cabin was interesting, the sloping dashboard being a key feature.*

■ LEFT *Lotus boosted the power of its four-cylinder engine by turbocharging it. Up to 264bhp was a remarkable output for a 2.2-litre engine.*

provided convincing performance for its day, but produced probably the best-handling Lotus yet. The five-speed gearbox was taken directly from the Citroën SM.

As it transpired, Giugiaro's clean-cut and simple shape would stand the test of time with honours. The interesting interior architecture was perhaps less

appealing over the longer term but, for its day, the Esprit was a state-of-the-art mid-engined sportscar.

Lotus kept abreast of the opposition's advances with constant developments. An S2 version with an integrated front spoiler appeared in 1978, and the S2.2 with an expanded 2.2-litre engine in 1980, the same year the spectacular

Esprit Turbo was launched. The 2.2-litre Turbo engine developed 210bhp, enough to force a much stiffer chassis with larger wheels and brakes and revised suspension, creating a peerless car in handling terms. The S3 of 1981 incorporated most of the Turbo chassis refinements and added a wraparound front bumper.

■ LEFT *All Esprit models were fast, and no car handled as well as an Esprit. This is a Series 3 model at full chat.*

■ LEFT *The Esprit proved to be a very long-lasting model for the Norfolk company.*

■ ABOVE *In its ultimate guise, the Esprit gained a V-eight engine and a phenomenal power-to-weight ratio.*

In this form the Esprit continued until 1987, when Lotus's in-house designer, Peter Stevens, effected a brilliant restyle of the bodywork, creating smoothed-off and more aerodynamic lines. At the same time, the chassis was stiffened and the gearbox switched to Renault's GTA. The popular Turbo survived in even more powerful guise, boasting up to 264bhp.

There was another restyle in 1993, when the nose and rear wing were reshaped, the interior was improved and power steering standardized. Two new models were launched: the S4S and the Sport 300 with its 302bhp engine (still from just 2.2 litres and four cylinders).

By 1996, the Esprit was 21 years old and still going strong, but it desperately needed some extra urge to compete with the best from Ferrari. Lotus developed a brand-new V-eight engine for the purpose, twin-turbocharged to produce a massive 349bhp. Fitted with a six-speed gearbox, the new Esprit V8 was a formidable performer, and looked set to continue to uphold the Lotus tradition for many years yet.

■ LEFT *In 1987, the Esprit got a major redesign by Peter Stevens, rounding off its edges and adding some length.*

■ BELOW *Despite its increasing age, the Esprit remained a competitive and very British sportscar.*

LOTUS ESPRIT (1975–)	
Engine	4/V-eight-cylinder
Capacity	1973–3179cc
Power	160–349bhp
Transmission	5/6-speed
Top speed	130–170mph (209–274kph)
No. built	9,150 (to end of 1996)

LOTUS

■ LEFT *The Elan powered its way into the sports history books with its amazing handling ability, which was all the more remarkable since this was Lotus's first-ever front-wheel-drive car.*

■ LOTUS ELAN

In the 1960s, the Elan name meant just one thing: the best-handling, most fun-to-drive small sportscar you could buy. When Lotus decided, in 1989, to revive the name on its first all-new car in 14 years, it was fully aware of the legacy it had to live up to. Thankfully, in all major areas, it succeeded in creating a worthy successor.

In conception, the new Elan was unlike anything Lotus had tried before, and for one reason: it had front-wheel drive. If traditional Lotus enthusiasts were nervous about this development, they had no need, for the Elan was probably the most competent handling car available. In some eyes it was too efficient, simply gripping the road tighter the more you asked of it and lacking the involvement of other Lotus cars.

Peter Stevens designed the stubby bodywork and ex-Formula 1 driver John Miles developed the interactive suspension. Lotus went to Isuzu in Japan for its engine – a 1.6-litre twin-cam unit in normally aspirated or turbocharged SE forms.

The Elan sold for a very reasonable price, too reasonable as it turned out, as Lotus lost money on each one sold. Yet sales were disappointing, mainly because a worldwide economic recession was beginning to bite and the near-simultaneous release of Mazda's Miata, which offered comparable performance at half the cost. Amid financial problems, Lotus was forced to abandon production after just two years.

A saviour appeared in the form of Bugatti, which bought Lotus from its parent company General Motors and in 1994, using existing components, embarked on a limited run of 800 additional S2 Elans. These featured some 100 changes, including better suspension, larger wheels, new seats and a better hood. Later, the Elan project was revived by Kia in Korea.

ABOVE *All black and red: the cockpit was completely geared towards making the driving experience as visceral as possible.*

LOTUS ELAN (1989–94)	
Engine	4-cylinder
Capacity	1588cc
Power	130–165bhp
Transmission	5-speed
Top speed	122–137mph (196–220kph)
No. built	4,655

■ LEFT *Peter Stevens created another masterpiece of design, no mean feat considering the very short wheelbase he had to work with.*

■ ABOVE *The stubby two-seater had an effective folding top to make it a practical year-round car.*

■ RIGHT *The first new Lotus for a decade was always going to be greeted with intense interest, and the Elise marked a true revolution in sportscar design with its extruded-aluminium chassis.*

■ LOTUS ELISE

Light weight was always Colin Chapman's very first priority when designing a new Lotus. After his death in 1982, Lotus engineers adhered to this principle, and in the Elise, which epitomised it, they produced a spiritual successor to the immortal Lotus 7.

The heart of the Elise, and the reason why it was so light, was its perfectly functional chassis. Breaking with Lotus tradition, it was a monocoque design formed from pieces of lightweight aluminium, literally stretched into shape and glued together. Even the brakes were aluminium composite. This was the secret of its lightness.

The suspension was so good it needed no anti-roll bars, and testers were unanimous in their praise: this was simply the finest handling car ever made.

While the 1989 Elan was front-engined and front-wheel drive, the Elise was mid-engined and rear-wheel drive, and all the more enjoyable for this change. The chosen engine was Rover's all-aluminium 1.8-litre K-series (as fitted to the MGF), complete with its gearbox. This provided all the performance it needed: after all the Elise was only about half the weight of a small family hatchback.

The best thing about it, though, was its price: at under £20,000 ($33,000) in the UK it was a bargain.

■ ABOVE *Leaving the aluminium chassis exposed in the cockpit was an inspired move, utterly in keeping with its role as a super-lightweight, no-frills sportscar.*

■ ABOVE *Thanks to extreme light weight, the Elise was a good performer despite its mild 120bhp engine: 0-60mph (0-96 kph) in 5.5 seconds was extraordinarily quick.*

LOTUS ELISE (1996–)	
Engine	4-cylinder
Capacity	1795cc
Power	120bhp @ 5500rpm
Transmission	5-speed
Top speed	124mph (200kph)
No. built	Still in production

OTHER MAKES

■ LAND-ROVER

After the Second World War, Britain needed a jeep-style all-rounder and the Willys Jeep was used as a template to create the Land-Rover in 1948. It quickly became an international legend, very tough and unassailable off-road. The same basic design remains in production today as the Defender, although Land-Rover branched out in 1970 with the sophisticated Range Rover, in the 1980s with the Discovery all-rounder, and in the 1990s with the smaller Freelander series.

■ LIGIER

French millionaire racing driver and ex-rugby international Guy Ligier decided to build his own sportscar in 1970. The JS designation was in memory of his friend, Jo Schlesser, killed racing in 1969. A pressed-steel platform was fitted with a glassfibre coupé body. As presented at the 1970 Paris Salon, it had a mid-mounted Ford Capri engine, but production cars had Citroën SM V-six engines. Ligier went on to make very successful Formula 1 racing cars and a range of top-selling microcars.

■ LINCOLN

Ford of America's premium brand is Lincoln, purveyors of limousines and the darling of American presidents. Its mainstay, the Continental, was by the 1970s obscenely bloated. Long after every other American marque had down-sized, Lincoln continued to offer "full-size" cars. By 1977, even Lincoln was offering an alternative with the luxury, compact Versailles, which did not do well. More successful were its big coupés such as the Mark VII and LSC, but overall Lincoln never matched the success of its main GM rival Cadillac.

MARCOS

■ MARCOS

The name Marcos was a composite of two illustrious characters in the world of specialist motoring, Jem Marsh and Frank Costin. The first model they created was an all-wooden sportscar, which was brilliant on the track (Jackie Stewart started off in one) but was so hideous that it acquired the nickname "ugly duckling".

Out of this unusual birth came the definitive Marcos in 1963, whose basic shape remains in production today. The

■ ABOVE *In the 1980s, Marcos's founder Jem Marsh began altering the basic coupé concept by, for example, introducing this convertible version.*

■ ABOVE *Enthusiasts respect the Marcos badge as one of the great British sportscar companies, with an impressive competition record and successful road-car range.*

■ ABOVE *It is an impressive fact that Marcos began producing this GT car in 1964, and it continues to be a popular new sportscar in its fourth decade.*

■ ABOVE *Aerodynamic and lightweight, all Marcos models were fast and furious, especially with the modifed Rover V-eight engines the company fitted from the mid-1980s.*

Adams brothers, Dennis and Peter, designed the new Marcos and, at its debut at the 1964 Racing Car Show, it stole the honours. A futuristic glassfibre body sat on the familiar Marcos wooden chassis.

The original intention had been to create an "all-new" car with its own tailor-made suspension, but financial constraints led to Triumph wishbones being used on the front, although a novel de Dion rear end with Triumph arms was

fitted. Even this, however, was later changed to a Ford live-axle set-up. Marcos cars used Ford, Volvo and Triumph engines.

Marcos's "pot-boiler" in the 1960s was the Mini-Marcos, a quite ugly little buzz-box whose main distinction lay in its being the only British car to finish the 1966 Le Mans 24-Hour Race. Powered by a Mini engine, it was cheap but crude and was still available new as late as 1994.

MARCOS GT (1964–)	
Engine	4/6/V-eight-cylinder
Capacity	1498–4999cc
Power	82–352bhp
Transmission	4/5-speed manual
Top speed	110–171mph (177–275kph)
No. built	Approx. 1,500 to date

■ RIGHT *There was no other car with a shape like that of the Marcos, which was at once muscular, individual and futuristic.*

■ ABOVE *Despite its extremely low profile, there was enough room to make the driver feel very comfortable. The seats were fixed and the pedals could move to fit the driver.*

Marcos underwent a temporary demise as a producer of cars in 1971. Marsh continued to provide servicing and parts for Marcos cars for ten more years, and then boldly relaunched the two seater in 1981 with a variety of Ford engines. In a world starved of sportscars, the Marcos met with immediate success, especially when Marsh installed a Rover V-eight engine to create the Mantula in 1983. Even more attractive was the drop-top Spyder model of 1985. All Marcos models shared the same basic shape as the classic Adams-penned

1800 of 1963, though the profile evolved with wider wheel arches, spoilers and fatter wheels and tyres.

In 1992, a new chapter was written with the arrival of the fully built Mantara, a totally new car with different front suspension and a more radical interpretation of the classic body shape. The Mantara had the option of a Rover 4.5-litre engine, giving a top speed of 160mph (257kph) and a 0–60mph (0–96kph) time under five seconds.

Even more spectacular was the 1994 LM series, the letters of its name hinting

at Marcos's re-entry into the Le Mans racing arena. Two versions were offered, the LM500 with a 4.0-litre V-eight engine and the LM600 with a 5.0-litre engine and 320bhp, enough to reach a cool 169mph (272kph).

In 1996, Marcos turned to Ford of America for the Mantis which had a quoted top speed of over 170mph (274kph) and a 0–60mph (0–96kph) time of 4.1 seconds. Ford's quad-cam V-eight engine, with its 352bhp of power, was described as "adequate for a car that weighs 1050kg (2316lb)"!

■ ABOVE *As the years progressed, Marcos cars developed wild arches and aerodynamic aids. This is a 1993 Mantara.*

■ RIGHT *In 1996, Marcos switched from Rover to a Ford V-eight engine in its Mantis. With a top speed of 171mph (275kph), this was now a true supercar.*

MASERATI

■ MASERATI BITURBO

By the 1980s, the once-great name of
Maserati was fading fast. Citroën had
taken an interest in 1968 but sold out to
De Tomaso in 1975, after which
Maserati's model development stagnated
and production dwindled. When a bold
new model was launched in 1981, the
intention was to boost Maserati
production. The Biturbo certainly did
that, but at the cost of permanently
denting Maserati's reputation.

While the car had its faults, the
main problem was that it didn't look or
feel like a real Maserati. In style it was
a dead-ringer for the BMW 3 Series;
but for its trident grille it looked
utterly anonymous.

If the Biturbo had one strength, it was
the performance delivered from the

twin-turbocharged multivalve V-six
engine. Producing 180bhp initially, it
was a very quick car if one had the
patience to wait for the turbo-lag to
disappear after the throttle was floored.
The original 2.0-litre engine (really
confected to exploit Italian tax rules)
was expanded to 2.5 litres in 1983, and
up to 2.8 litres in 1987, by which time
power output had reached 224bhp.

Its price and badge made a quick
killing for owners De Tomaso. In
America especially, the Biturbo sold in
very large numbers in the booming 80s.
This was a quick route into sharp-suited
Italian haute couture, especially in
ostentatious open-top Spyder form.

Its oft-quoted shortcomings included
evil handling, especially in the wet,
cramped rear-seat accommodation and
an interior of dubious taste, crowned as
it was by a huge clock and acres of lush
wood. Owners also found themselves
stranded by unreliable engines and

■ ABOVE *The appeal
of the Biturbo range
was extended with
the launch of a 425
four-door-saloon
(sedan) version
in 1983.*

■ LEFT *The maze of
plumbing betrays the
technology that gave
the Biturbo its
name: two
turbochargers. They
boosted out 180bhp
but suffered from
turbo lag.*

MASERATI BITURBO (1981–91)	
Engine	V-six cylinder
Capacity	1996–2790cc
Power	180–241bhp
Transmission	5-speed manual
Top speed	132–143mph (212–240kph)
No. built	Approx. 40,000

■ OPPOSITE *The world was plainly ready for a compact sports saloon with a Maserati badge, as the popularity of the Biturbo proved throughout the 1980s.*

■ BELOW *Later Biturbo models were badged 222, 224 (illustrated here) and 228. These were even more powerful than the early cars.*

■ ABOVE *Perhaps the most desirable of the Biturbo models was the fully convertible Spyder. It offered the same huge performance, open-topped fun and seating for four adults.*

distinctly cheesed off all round by rather poor craftsmanship.

Perhaps the redeeming feature of the Biturbo was that it put Maserati back on the map. It sold well enough to re-establish a fading name, and it did give rise to a bewildering profusion of follow-up models. These included a four-door version variously called the 420/425/430, a Spyder convertible, and the second-generation 2.22 and 2.24 (which lost the Biturbo label). Vastly superior were the stunningly fast Karif, Shamal and Ghibli of the 1990s, whose heritage was clearly traceable back to the first Biturbo but otherwise had almost nothing in common with it.

When Ferrari assumed overall control of Maserati in 1997, quality took a quantum leap in the right direction and the bad old days were forgotten. The Biturbo can be seen as the model that delivered Maserati safely into its new owner's hands.

■ ABOVE *Sumptuous leather and rich wood was a Maserati hallmark, and made the cabin feel very special. The dash was dominated by Maserati's trademark oval clock.*

■ RIGHT *The smart Italian clothing stood the Biturbo in good stead for many years, although some Maserati aficionados bemoaned a certain flash-in-the-pan flavour.*

MAZDA

■ MAZDA RX-7

Mazda will go down in history as the staunch defender of Wankel's rotary engine, and as the company which finally sorted its problems out. Long after pioneer NSU had bitten the dust, Mazda pursued the rotary ideal with a whole string of models, including saloons (sedans), coupés and sportscars.

Mazda had the courage to realize the inherent strengths of the rotary engine. The design was very compact and lightweight, it could run to extremely

■ ABOVE *The heart of the RX-7 was its rotary engine. Long after other manufacturers had abandoned it as a poor idea, Mazda proved it was possible to make it a success.*

■ BELOW *The second-generation RX-7 was softer, more practical, less characterful and more comfortable, but still had rotary power.*

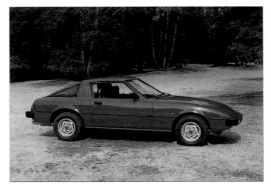

■ ABOVE *Mazda's RX-7 sportscar was highly respected in enthusiast circles. Its smart shape, speed, technology and character were sharply focused.*

■ LEFT *Although the raw performance of the first-generation RX-7 may not have been high-ranking, its cornering ability certainly was.*

high revs and was smoother than any other four-stroke engine. Its biggest fault was a propensity for drinking fuel.

The other original major concern was reliability. The engine depended on the integrity of the tips of the rotating triangle, which span around inside the combustion chamber. These tended to wear quickly and cause running difficulties. Modern technology finally addressed this problem (Mazda certainly had it cured during the life cycle of its RX-7) but by then the make's poor reputation was firmly established.

■ LEFT *Advanced materials and technology made the third-generation RX-7 an extremely rapid and enjoyable car.*

In later years, Mazda reserved the rotary engine for its range-topping coupés and sportscars. The RX-7 was an undoubted classic. For its day (it was launched in 1978), it was a unique blend of style and talent.

The centre of the magical RX-7 equation was the engine. Charismatic, sweet-running and powerful, there was nothing else like it. It may not have been overly fast, with a top speed of 120mph (193kph) and 0–60mph (0–96kph) in 8.6 seconds, but it was entertaining – except for a tendency to back-fire. When taken around bends there was little to fault the RX-7's

■ ABOVE *Japan had learned from Europe's best, and the latest RX-7's interior oozed class and purpose.*

■ BELOW *In 1992, the RX-7 evolved into a real supercar, with high performance now top of the agenda. 237bhp was very healthy for a car of its price.*

enthusiasm, and in character it was pure sportscar. If you wanted more performance you could take your RX-7 to a specialist like TWR, which offered a potent turbocharged conversion – and many customers did.

The RX-7's shark-nose coupé style was distinctive and, with the pop-up headlamps down, extremely clean.

■ ABOVE *The more cosseting interior of the 1986-92 RX-7 reflected its move up-market.*

Although it had a pair of rear seats, they were so small that this was essentially a two-seater. The first cars were quite starkly equipped, but gradually refinements like electric windows and a spoiler were introduced.

The second-generation RX-7 of 1986 was larger, heavier and softer, far less of a sportscar and more of a boulevard cruiser (especially in soft-top form, a body style never offered on the first RX-7). By 1992, the third-generation RX-7 had catapulted Mazda back into the sportscar league with a twin-turbo engine, an advanced and extremely attractive body structure and bristling performance.

Neither really duplicated the original purity of the first RX-7, which ranks as one of the most successful sportscars ever, with almost half a million of the first generation sold.

MAZDA RX-7 (1978–86)	
Engine	Twin-rotor Wankel
Capacity	2 × 573cc
Power	105–135bhp
Transmission	5-speed manual 3-speed auto
Top speed	113–125mph (182–201kph)
No. built	474,565

Mazda

■ MAZDA MX-5

In the 1980s, sportscars went completely out of fashion, not just passé but completely dead. All the great open sportscars were stamped on: MG, Triumph TR, Fiat Spider; only the Alfa Spider could be said to have kept the spark alight, and then only just. Against this background, Mazda made a courageous decision: it would single-handedly engineer the rebirth of the sportscar.

That 1989 decision was bold but it paid off handsomely. Other manufacturers may have decided that sportscars were no longer profitable, but the consumer had different ideas. The

■ ABOVE *Simple in style, the MX-5 exploited the rear-wheel-drive two-seater-roadster style abandoned by virtually every other major manufacturer.*

■ LEFT *The 1.8-litre engine was modest, perhaps, but just right for a car that was designed as an accessible small sportscar.*

■ LEFT *At speed the MX-5 impressed all who drove it. It was snappy, sharp around corners, responsive, yet refined.*

■ ABOVE *There were no frills in the instrument layout and choice of materials. The inspiration came from classic sportscars such as the MGB.*

world still wanted to drive sportscars, and Mazda got the confection absolutely right in its MX-5.

Here was a cheap two-seater open-topped car with a front-mounted engine and rear-wheel drive. To many onlookers this sounded rather like an MGB, an impression reinforced by the compact, curvaceous shape. Where the MX-5 excelled – and dispelled any criticism of plagiarism – was in its handling. Unlike the antiquated manners of the MGB, the

MX-5 was superbly modern: just the right degree of handling aplomb was engineered in for safety and fun.

This was a classic design in which everything was somehow right, from the evocative rear lights and front pop-ups to the simplicity of the specification and the enjoyment factor. Underneath it was brilliantly engineered, with engine, gearbox and final drive carried on a separate subframe, and double-wishbone suspension for crisp handling.

The interior was kept sparse in the best sporting traditions: little in the way of electronic gizmos and a great sense of quality and simplicity. The only criticisms were over-light power-steering and a lack of performance from the 1.6-litre engine.

In Japan, the car was launched as the Eunos Roadster, in Europe it was the Mazda MX-5 and in America it was the Miata. In each market, the model became a legend. Thanks to its very

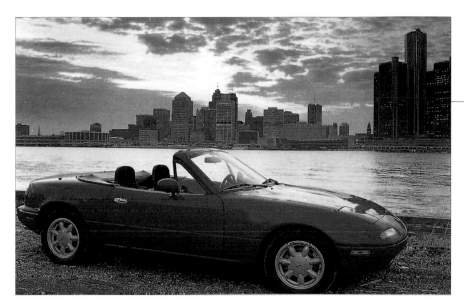

reasonable price, it was accessible to many drivers and it sold in vast numbers. Admittedly, it had little competition, but there is no denying its essential brilliance. In any case, in many markets the MX-5 sold best in its later years when there was plenty of competition from the likes of the MGF, Fiat Barchetta and BMW Z3. The plain fact was that the little Mazda paved the way for everyone else: it really brought about the renaissance of the sportscar.

Very little changed during its career. The addition of safety features such as side-impact bars and airbags increased its weight, so the MX-5 got a 1.8-litre fuel-injected engine in 1993; a 1.6-litre model was kept going as a bargain entry-level model.

It took until 1997 for a replacement for the MX-5 to arrive, and it precisely duplicated the format of this ultra-successful car. By then the MX-5 had become the world's favourite sportscar, with a production tally over 400,000.

■ ABOVE *Two comfortable seats, an open roof and an open road – one very simple formula for success.*

■ LEFT *A big splash is the only way to describe the MX-5's impact. Within a few years, numerous manufacturers had launched their own junior sportscars on the back of the MX-5's success.*

MAZDA MX-5 (1989–97)	
Engine	4-cylinder
Capacity	1597–1840cc
Power	90–131bhp
Transmission	5-speed manual 4-speed auto
Top speed	108–122mph (174–196kph)
No. built	Over 400,000

■ BELOW *The McLaren F1 laid the strongest claim to be the world's ultimate car. Its provenance from a World Championship Formula 1 team was decisive.*

MᶜLAREN

■ MᶜLAREN F1

It's not every designer or engineer who has the chance to build the ultimate car, with absolutely no expense spared. Perhaps Bugatti did it with the extravagant Royale in the 1930s, but few in the industry could argue that Gordon Murray's McLaren F1 was anything but the ultimate road-going car.

A former chief Formula 1 designer at Brabham, then at Woking-based McLaren, Murray had a burning but unfulfilled passion to build a machine that qualified as the fastest, most involving road car yet made – and, of

■ ABOVE *The purchase of an F1 was reserved for the privileged few, since its price (£635,000 ($1,070,000)) was vastly higher than that of any other car ever made.*

■ ABOVE *Surrounding the specially designed BMW V-twelve 6.0-litre engine was a hand-finished film of pure gold, chosen for its heat-dissipating qualities.*

course, the most expensive. Yet it would also have to be a car you could happily drive into town.

Ideas at McLaren began crystallizing during 1988, and in March 1989 Murray announced his plans to the public. Murray was in charge of design and development, while Lotus stylist Peter Stevens would pen the car's shape, and BMW's Motorsport division had agreed to design an all-new V-twelve engine from scratch. Everything revolved around Murray's ideal precepts, such as the innovative three-seater cabin with

MCLAREN F1 (1993–97)	
Engine	V-twelve-cylinder
Capacity	6064cc
Power	609-627bhp @ 7400rpm
Transmission	6-speed
Top speed	231mph (372kph)
No. built	100

■ LEFT *The stunningly simple yet aggressive shape was designed by Peter Stevens. The bodywork was realized in exotic carbonfibre.*

■ ABOVE *Project creator Gordon Murray insisted that there should be three seats, the central one occupied by the driver. The "arrowhead" formation proved practical.*

the driver sitting in the middle ahead of the two passengers.

Another crucial factor was the target weight: an unbelievable 2205lb (1000kg) (Ferrari's F40 weighed 2720lb (1235kg) and Jaguar's XJ220 weighed 3240lb (1470kg)). Every detail was under scrutiny to see if it could be made lighter.

With no less than 627bhp on tap from the 6064cc BMW V-twelve engine, the truly explosive performance which Murray had been aiming for became a reality. Ex-Formula 1 driver Jonathan Palmer flew to the Nardo test track in Italy in August 1993 and, in the searing heat, he drove the F1 at an incredible 231mph (372kph). Tests betrayed more amazing figures: 0–60mph (0–96kph) in 3.2 seconds, 0–100mph (0–161kph) in 6.3 seconds and 30–70mph

■ ABOVE *Every component on the F1 was designed especially for its role, from the wheels and tyres to the hi-fi system. Everything was engineered down to a weight.*

(48–113kph) in just over 2 seconds. Such incredible performance made the F1 almost invincible on the track: an F1 GTR came first in virtually every GT Endurance race it entered, and the F1 was triumphant at Le Mans in 1995.

Then there was the cost: no less than £635,000 ($1,070,000), reflecting the huge development budget, ultra-high

technology and the fact that, initially, each one took 6,000 man-hours to build. Then there were all the little touches that made the F1 so special, like the gold-insulated engine bay, the unbelievably complex sound system, total leeway for individual colour choice and tailored luggage. If you had car problems, McLaren would jet out a mechanic on the next available flight.

The first customer car was finished on Christmas Eve 1993, and the last one of a total of exactly 100 cars – far short of the initial target of 300 – was completed in 1997. There could hardly be a more exclusive car than this.

■ ABOVE *The high-tech gauges said it all: with a dial going up to 240mph (386kph).*

■ RIGHT *The F1 LM was a limited-edition model painted in the racer and race-car constructor Bruce McLaren's racing orange and fitted with a rear spoiler, special wheels and modified bodywork.*

MERCEDES

■ BELOW *While other roadsters in the 1970s became bloated or disappeared altogether, Mercedes-Benz produced the superbly strong SL series.*

■ MERCEDES-BENZ SL

SL has traditionally denoted Mercedes-Benz's sporting models, and the two letters were always taken to mean Sport and Leicht (lightweight). The first SL was the 1954 300SL Gullwing coupé, and the most popular were the "pagoda roof" models produced between 1963 and 1971.

When it came to replacing these classic SLs, Mercedes-Benz took an important step into its own future in 1972. Gone were the stacked headlamps of all

MERCEDES-BENZ SL (1989–)	
Engine	6/V-eight-/V-twelve-cylinder
Capacity	2799–5987cc
Power	190–389bhp
Transmission	5-speed manual 4/5-speed auto
Top speed	138–155mph (222–249kph)
No. built	Still in production

■ LEFT *In one of its ultimate W107 series guises, the 500SL seen here, the drop-top Merc had a fabulous 241bhp 5.0-litre V-eight engine.*

previous Mercedes models, replaced by strong horizontal rectangular units (US models received a pair of round lamps) and wrap-around indicators, anticipating future themes on its saloons (sedans).

Viewed objectively, the so-called

W107 SL was an absolute classic, which lasted in production for almost 20 years. It was quite a different car, expanded in every way over the "pagoda roof" SL and considerably improved in safety matters.

The new SL was initially powered by

Mercedes-Benz's 3.5-litre V-eight, or its even more powerful 4.5-litre V-eight. Modernized suspension featured a semi-trailing-arm rear-end, and there was standard power-steering, and a popular optional automatic gearbox. From 1974, the entry-level 280SL was launched in Continental Europe (but not in the UK or the US), sporting the twin-cam six-cylinder engine from the 280E.

The SL Series was revamped in 1980 as a new range of engines slotted in. The full list during the 1980s was: 280SL, 300SL, 380SL, 420SL, 500SL and 560SL. A second SL sub-species was the longer-wheelbase fixed-head SLC series produced from 1972, which were proper four-seaters and probably the best grand tourers made in the 1970s.

■ RIGHT *With a lengthened wheelbase and a fixed roof, the SL transformed into the Grand Touring SLC four-seater, a strong contender in its day for the accolade of best car in the world.*

By the late 1980s, the SL had lost its sporting edge, and Mercedes-Benz aimed to address that problem with a brand-new SL series in 1989. The result was one of the best cars Mercedes-Benz ever produced. It looked wonderfully balanced, drove like a sportscar or a tourer, depending on your mood, and had all the qualities one would expect of a top-flight model from Stuttgart.

It was launched with a choice of two engines: the 300SL six-cylinder (offered in 190bhp standard and 231bhp twin-cam forms), and the deeply impressive 500SL V-eight. Naturally, there was a power-operated soft-top and a wind deflector to keep your hair style in order, and one extraordinary novelty was a hidden roll-over bar, which popped up when the car reached a certain angle,

■ ABOVE *The SL heritage stretches right back, through these five generations, to the celebrated 300SL of the 1950s.*

■ LEFT *In addition to a very effective electric folding roof, an important safety measure was a roll-over bar, which automatically popped up in case of an accident.*

■ BELOW *With an optional hardtop fitted, the SL became an attractive and snug coupé.*

telling an on-board computer that a serious accident was imminent. Another interesting option on the V-eight was its speed-sensitive suspension.

Mercedes-Benz's most expensive car arrived in 1992 in the V-twelve-powered 600SL. With its 48-valve 389bhp engine and automatic damping it was crushingly quick, yet still superbly refined. The ultimate version was the six-litre V-eight AMG-tweaked SL60 with body kit, 381bhp and huge 18in (45.7cm) wheels.

■ ABOVE LEFT *When it came to replacing the SL in 1989, Mercedes produced its best incarnation yet. Low-slung and elegant, it epitomized the luxury roadster form.*

■ RIGHT *Mercedes interiors are nearly always sober affairs, with solidity and logic given higher priority than design flair.*

MERCEDES

■ MERCEDES-BENZ SLK

In the parlance of Mercedes-Benz, "K" signals "*Kompakt*", and indeed the SLK was a smaller breed of bargain-priced Mercedes SL sportscar, and the first junior Mercedes sportscar since the 190SL of the late 1950s. It was a perfect foil to the new Porsche Boxster and BMW Z3 roadster, selling to a new kind of customer for Mercedes: a telling statistic is that over half of those who ordered an SLK had never had a Mercedes before.

■ ABOVE *A brilliantly effective solid roof folded at the touch of a button under the boot (trunk) lid. The lid would then open the opposite way to permit luggage storage.*

■ BELOW *In its most sporting guise, the 230 Kompressor pictured here, the SLK was a very rapid sportscar, up to 143mph (230kph) being possible.*

■ ABOVE *Mercedes-Benz could hardly have produced a more desirable junior sportscar than the SLK, its first attempt at this growing market. With the top raised, it looked and felt like a proper coupé.*

To cut costs, the engine and driveline components were shared with the C Class saloons (sedans), the brakes came from the E Class, and seats were bought in from Recaro. The headlights were unique but moulded in plastic. Expensive magnesium structural components were used, but they saved space and enhanced safety.

The car's party trick was an exotic electric roof. In 25 seconds, the SLK's solid Vario roof arched into the air, folded itself in two and carefully stowed itself away in the boot (trunk) before a metal cover snapped shut. The sequence even wound the windows down for you. It worked just as well in reverse, transforming the SLK back into a draught-free coupé, and you didn't even have to clip the roof on to the windscreen edge. Mercedes promised that the electric motors and hydraulic rams were good for at least 20,000 repeat performances.

Inside, the car's cabin was highly styled with embracing bucket seats, and carbonfibre-look cladding on the dashboard and white back-lit dials sunk into chrome-edged portholes.

This was a rear-drive car but, with
anti-lock brakes and traction control,
only the reckless could provoke the back
of the SLK out of line. Its ride and
roadholding balance were superbly fluid,
and, as with all Mercedes automatics,
you could flick the shift down for a faster
getaway or change-down for a corner.
With the 193bhp supercharged four-
cylinder engine, the car's top speed was
more than 140mph (225kph), with
0–60mph (0–96kph) in 7 seconds, while
there was a cheaper non-supercharged
model, too.

The SLK proved amazingly popular,
with orders backed up until the end of
the century: it seemed that Mercedes's
biggest problem with the SLK was
building enough of them.

■ ABOVE *Detail of the ingenious electric hood
(top) operation.*

■ ABOVE LEFT *The word Kompressor on the
cylinder-head cover indicates the presence of
a supercharger in the 2.3-litre engine, good
enough for 193bhp.*

■ ABOVE RIGHT *Especially classy was the
interior treatment, with carbonfibre-style
overlay, white dials apparently hewn out of
the dash and a classic Mercedes steering wheel.*

MERCEDES-BENZ SLK (1996–)	
Engine	4-cylinder
Capacity	1998–2295cc
Power	136–193bhp
Transmission	5-speed manual or auto
Top speed	126–143mph (203–230kph)
No. built	Still in production

MG

■ MG RV8

MG is without doubt one of the great sportscar names. Sadly, however, that name was squandered by British Leyland, its parent company in the 1970s, and its once-great sportscar line was left to wither on the vine until the compromised, outdated MGB shuddered out of existence in 1980.

Although the MG badge survived on performance versions of some Austin cars, this seemed to be the end for the MG sportscar. MG enthusiasts never forgot the "B", however, and a huge industry quickly grew up around

■ LEFT *Thirty years after the MGB's birth, Rover revived its seminal sportscar and gave it a thorough revamp and a V-eight engine to create the MG RV8.*

■ BELOW *The gadget-laden RV8 interior, rife with gauges, was a much more cosseting location than the stark old MGB.*

■ LEFT *No MGB-manufactured roadster had ever had a V-eight engine. The 1990s version was engineered to accept Rover's 3.9-litre Range Rover unit which developed 190bhp.*

■ ABOVE *After more than a decade in a wilderness devoid of sports models, the MG badge was revived to the cheers of enthusiasts.*

restoring this enduring classic. Even Austin-Rover got involved in 1989 when its Heritage division went into production with brand-new replacement MGB bodyshells.

The Rover Group realized that the MG badge still had tremendous potential, and it set about a relaunch of the brand. Its main aim was to produce an all-new mid-engined car (which became the MGF), but almost as an appetizer it decided to produce a radically updated MGB for the 30th

anniversary of its birth. Not only would it look different, it would have an engine that the drop-top "B" had never had – the venerable Rover V-eight – and would come with the name MG RV8.

The idea came about because its Heritage division had the capacity to make a respectable number of bodyshells (about 15 per week). Although the new design was much modified, many of the original pressings were unaltered, so it made sense logistically to do this.

■ BELOW *Always exclusive, the MG RV8 found many homes in export markets such as Japan.*

■ RIGHT *Typically British in every way, the interior reeked of walnut capping, rich leather and chrome detailing.*

MG RV8 (1992–96)	
Engine	V-eight-cylinder
Capacity	3946cc
Power	190bhp @ 4750rpm
Transmission	5-speed
Top speed	135mph (217kph)
No. built	n/a

■ BELOW *It may have shown its age in action, but there was no denying that the RV8 had strong performance and great presence.*

Rover stylists set about beefing up the old "B". The bonnet (hood), boot lid (trunk) and doors were kept the same but the rest of the bodywork was retouched, notably having wider wheel-arches, new bumpers, faired-in headlamps and skirts. Its more purposeful look was boosted by very smart spoked alloy wheels and wide tyres.

The basics of the mechanical package remained rather antique, including a live rear axle suspended on leaf springs. Rover's team tried to improve handling by widening the track and fitting Koni dampers, but there was no escaping the age of the design.

The best news was the installation of Rover's aluminium 3.9-litre V-eight engine, not only decently powerful but boasting a huge spread of torque. A claimed 0–60mph (0–96kph) figure of six seconds was backed up by a top speed of 135mph (217kph).

The interior was classically British: walnut veneer for the dashboard and door cappings, chromed door handles, lots of leather trim and a plethora of small gauges. The lack of such modern-day gadgets as electric windows and mirrors and power-steering merely

seemed to add to the olde worlde aura.

Its launch price of just over £25,000 ($42,000) looked good, and immediately there was a long queue of customers. Admittedly, since the RV8 was hardly at the cutting edge of sportscar technology, the main appeal was nostalgia and the fact that production would be very limited, but the RV8 was always in demand right up until its demise in 1996.

MG

■ MGF

Those who thought that the MG sportscar was dead eventually got the news they had been hoping for: the MG RV8 retro sportscar would be a precursor to an all-new, thoroughly modern MG. This would be a car as the MGB would have evolved, not a throwback to an antique age. For sure, all the qualities which made an MG special would be carefully dialled into the design equation, but this was meant to be a cutting-edge, affordable sportscar for the 1990s.

When it was launched at the 1995 Geneva Motor Show, the new MGF did not disappoint the crowds. Parent company Rover decided to opt for a centrally mounted engine because it gave the best handling potential, and in that respect the MGF was triumphant. Every tester returned with stories of tenacious grip, fluid cornering and an impressively stiff bodyshell.

The shape was tailored to appeal. Unambiguously modern, it took the theme of the MG grille and extrapolated a smooth, purposeful profile. Some thought it perhaps too anodyne, too close to the Japanese school of design, but no one questioned its effectiveness.

Inside, the traditional MG cues were more abundant but still not over-embellished. Even the moulded MG badges were restrained. The general feel was very classy, with white dials, leather steering wheel and attractive trim.

For its power, the MGF drew on the acclaimed K-series engine in 1.8-litre form. Two versions were offered: the 120bhp 1.8i and the powerful 145bhp 1.8i VVC, which could reach 60mph (96kph) from rest in just seven seconds thanks to its Variable Valve Control

■ LEFT *In 1997, a heavily modified MGF called the EXF was driven at the Bonneville salt flats in America to a top speed of 217mph (349kph) – the fastest MG ever.*

■ ABOVE *With the VVC engine, the MGF was capable of 0–60mph (0–96kph) in seven seconds and a top speed of 130mph (209kph).*

MGF (1995–)	
Engine	4-cylinder
Capacity	1795cc
Power	120–145bhp
Transmission	5-speed manual
Top speed	120–130mph (193–209kph)
No. built	Still in production

■ LEFT *Sportscar enthusiasts around the world applauded the official rebirth of the MG sportscar when the MGF was launched.*

■ OPPOSITE *In 1.8i VVC form, the MGF was equipped with special five-spoke alloy wheels, power-steering, ABS and – most importantly – a more powerful 145bhp engine. An optional hardtop was available.*

■ BELOW *The cockpit of the MGF was very sporting (white gauges, sports steering wheel, attractive upholstery) and was applauded for not overdoing the number of MG badges.*

engine mapping. The VVC also added standard power-steering, anti-lock brakes and unique alloy wheels.

A waiting-list immediately sprang up for the MG in Europe and Japan, with most buyers wanting the VVC version. The average age of an MGF buyer was over 50, but this came down as the model grew in acceptance

■ ABOVE *The MGF may have looked back to the MGB for its grille, but there the similarity ended. The mid-engined layout was thoroughly modern and delivered one of the best driving experiences around.*

OTHER MAKES

■ MATRA

With a background in aerospace and weapons, Marcel Chassagny's Mécanique Aviation Traction (or Matra) also became a car-maker when, in 1964, it took over René Bonnet's sportscar operation. The bizarre 530 followed the Djet in 1967 and, in 1970, Chrysler-Simca took the firm over. The 1973 three-seats-abreast Bagheera used a Simca engine. After the post-Peugeot take-over, another name change in 1979 to Talbot-Matra coincided with the launch of the Murena coupé and Rancho estate. Renault acquired Matra in the 1980s and inherited an MPV (minivan) prototype that Matra had developed (the Espace, which Matra manufactured).

■ MERCURY

Mercury was born in 1939 as a species of Ford that slotted in below Lincoln. Its 1970s offerings mirrored Ford's, the highlights being the Cougar and Marquis coupés and the Capri (initially a German Ford import, later a clone of the Mustang II). In the 1980s, Mercury's success was bolstered by solid mid-range virtues and the occasional character car like the Capri convertible.

■ MINI

Alec Issigonis's masterstroke Mini started off life in 1959 with Austin and Morris badging. After ten years in production, the Mini was launched as a marque in its own right under British Leyland. The legendary Mini-Cooper was launched in 1961 and production ended in 1971. Mini became Britain's best-selling marque in the 1970s (over five million made). Packaging included larger wheels in 1984, a Cooper relaunch in 1990, 1275cc engine only from 1992 and fuel injection from 1996. The Mini brand was relaunched in 1996 as a prelude to an all-new, 21st-century Mini.

■ MITSUBISHI

Japan's Number Three marque has always been very conservative and sold better in the domestic market than abroad (where it was called Colt for many years). The most interesting Mitsubishis were the 1970–6 Galant GTO coupé (a Japanese Mustang), the 1976–85 Sapporo, the 1982–90 Starion and the Car of the Year award-winning 1994 FTO coupé. Mitsubishi also pioneered direct petrol injection technology and established a European co-venture with Volvo in Holland.

■ MORGAN

Morgan is a unique company. It alone continues to make a car that looks and behaves exactly the same as it did 50 years ago: separate chassis, sliding pillar suspension, ash frame and hand-made bodywork. H.F.S. Morgan started production of three-wheelers in 1910 at Malvern, England, and this was continued by his son Peter and grandson Charles. Four-wheelers were made from 1936. The best Morgan was the Rover V-eight-engined Plus 8, made from 1968. Morgan has always thrived: there is a long waiting-list for all of the 450 cars it can produce per year – still in the factory where the cars have been made for over 75 years.

■ MORRIS

In 1912, William Morris (later Lord Nuffield), started building cars in Cowley, Oxford, and Morris Motors became one of the Britain's biggest companies. It grew up to become the Nuffield empire, incorporating names such as MG, Riley and Wolseley. In 1952, the group united with Austin to form the British Motor Corporation, then Europe's biggest car concern. By the 1970s, Morris was earmarked as the conventionally engineered badge. The last Morris was the lack-lustre Ital, which died in 1984.

NISSAN

■ NISSAN 300ZX

Nissan's Z series sportscars date back to the classic Goertz-styled 240Z coupé, one of the world's most successful sportscars. By the 1980s, however, the original ideals of light weight, sharp styling and quick responses had been lost in the bloated, suburban ZX of 1984–9, which was obviously meant for posing rather than driving.

That whole dead end was smashed through with the stunning new 300ZX of 1990. *Autocar* magazine called it "Japan's first-ever supercar" after it recorded a top speed of 155mph (250kph) and a 0–60mph (0–96kph) time of just 5.6 seconds. That was

■ ABOVE *The cabin could have been mistaken for that of a prestige European sportscar. The two-plus-two seating arrangement was, however, rather cramped.*

courtesy of a 300bhp twin-turbocharged three-litre engine with variable-valve timing sited up front and driving the rear wheels.

Even more impressive was the suspension, a complex multi-link set-up with HICAS four-wheel steering which automatically adapted itself to the driver's style. This enhanced turn-in, improved grip and stability and helped provide magnificently neutral cornering, although caution was required in very wet weather.

The interior looked and felt better than most Japanese cars, although it was rather cramped. Lift the T-bar roof off, however, and you had a feeling of open-air motoring.

Like the styling, the character of the 300ZX was up front, and customers appreciated its fine value for money and

■ ABOVE *Japan's first supercar was an accurate assessment of Nissan's bold new 300ZX of 1989.*

rewarding attributes. In America a convertible version won even more friends, but in Britain the 300ZX was suddenly dropped in 1994 after falling foul of emissions legislation. Elsewhere it continued for another two years.

NISSAN 300ZX (1989–1996)	
Engine	V-six-cylinder
Capacity	2560cc
Power	300bhp @ 6400rpm
Transmission	5-speed manual 4-speed auto
Top speed	155mph (250kph)
No. built	Not known

■ FAR LEFT *An attractive fully convertible 300ZX was sold in certain markets such as the USA. This model was selected as the PPG circuit Pace Car in America.*

■ LEFT *The twin-turbocharged 3.0 litre V-six engine developed 300bhp. This was a very sophisticated unit boasting variable valve timing.*

■ RIGHT *The normal Skyline was a saloon (sedan) car from the middle of Nissan's range, but the GT-R with its spoilers and skirts was a technological firecracker of a fast car.*

■ NISSAN SKYLINE GT-R

Skyline is a badge which Nissan has used since 1955, more recently denoting its more sporty upper-medium saloon (sedan) range. Everything changed in the 1989 eighth-generation Skyline, however, for a brand-new model joined the line up: the legendary GT-R.

With its deep front air dam, wide wheel-arches and tall rear spoiler, this two-door saloon (sedan) looked as if it would go fast. The 2.6-litre twin turbo six-cylinder engine made sure that it did, all 280bhp of it ensuring sizzling performance, such as 0–60mph (0–96kph) in five seconds and a top speed of 153mph (246kph).

That was just the start of the GT-R's wizardry. It also boasted four wheel drive with sensors on each wheel to control the split of torque front-to-rear, plus active suspension and four-wheel steering, which adjusted the angle of the

NISSAN SKYLINE GT-R (1989–)	
Engine	6-cylinder
Capacity	2569cc
Power	280bhp @ 6800rpm
Transmission	5-speed manual
Top speed	153mph (246kph)
No. built	Still in production

rear wheels according to the pressure being exerted on them. The result was that the GT-R pulled through corners amazingly quickly and safely while the excitement of piloting it was undiminished. It's little wonder that a GT-R recorded the fastest time ever for any road-going car around the legendary Nürburgring circuit in Germany.

In 1994, the next generation GT-R arrived, looking smoother and more rounded but with no loss of character. Initially sold only in Japan and Australia, it became a UK market debutante in 1997 with a price tag of £50,000 ($84,000).

■ LEFT *A GT-R famously recorded the fastest time ever for a production car around the Nürburgring in Germany: it was the only such car to go round in under eight minutes.*

OTHER MAKES

■ OLDSMOBILE

Born in 1897, Oldsmobile is America's oldest name-plate and part of the General Motors combine. By 1975 it was a middle-class luxury leader with a conservative slant, although models like the Starfire coupé and front-wheel-drive Toronado were more adventurous. Gradually, most of Oldsmobile's own model range declined into badge engineering, but unique cars such as the Cutlass and Aurora kept the flame burning.

■ OPEL

Opel has been General Motors' German wing since 1929. It relied on volume sales of medium-class cars like the Olympia, Rekord and Kapitän before moving into the small car arena with the 1962 Kadett. In the 1970s, Opel's strength lay in producing good-looking cars such as the Manta, GT and Commodore, while the 1973 Kadett was a true world car. British Vauxhall and German Opel products converged so that, by the 1980s, the differences were in the grilles and wheel-trims only.

■ LEFT *If 280bhp was too little for you, the GT-R provided the ideal basis for extreme tuning for road and track. Power outputs were known to go as high as 1200bhp.*

PANTHER

■ PANTHER

Panther is one of the most unusual companies in motoring history. In the 1970s, it became one of the most spectacularly successful British specialist manufacturers with a startlingly wide range of products.

Founded by Robert Jankel in 1972, Panther Westwinds started life with pastiches of bygone classics. The J72 was the first, a copy of the pre-war SS100 using Jaguar engines. The hand-built J72 sold to the rich and famous, including the film star Liz Taylor, for it certainly wasn't cheap, retailing at almost twice the price of an E-Type Jaguar.

Its next car was the 1974 De Ville, a creation of unrestrained opulence, with vaguely Bugatti Royale lines and superb craftsmanship. Mechanically, the De Ville was all Jaguar XJ12, including its suspension. In 1976, came the two-door De Ville Convertible, famous for being the most expensive car on British price lists – and the motorcar star of the film *101 Dalmatians*.

The concept behind Panther's 1975 Rio was quite sound: to create a small, economical car with the finish and luxury of a Rolls-Royce. In the troubled fuel crisis days of 1975, it looked

■ ABOVE *This is the interior of the J72, a feast of walnut and leather in the best neo-classic traditions.*

promising but suffered from comparisons with the car on which it was based, the Triumph Dolomite, which cost a third of the price. In commercial terms, the Rio was a complete flop and perhaps deserved a better fate.

■ ABOVE *Panther Westwinds made its living producing hand-built pastiches of a bygone era of motoring. The Kallista vaguely recalled the 1930s.*

■ ABOVE *Acres of chrome dazzled for effect on the nose of the De Ville. The hand-crafted coachbuilder's art was fostered at Panther.*

Not so the Lima, Panther's "car for the masses", which sold very well. The recipe was simple: a 1930s-style two-seater open glassfibre body on a strengthened Vauxhall Magnum floorpan, including the Magnum's engine, gearbox, suspension, steering and brakes.

Its successor was the 1982 Kallista. This used all-Ford components, including Cortina double-wishbone front suspension and a Capri live rear axle, and the revised bodywork was aluminium. It was not particularly quick, but was more roomy, more refined and better-handling than the Lima. It sold very healthily.

Apart from the incredible six-wheeled

■ LEFT *Panther's most extravagant car was the De Ville, a huge Bugatti-inspired device using Jaguar parts. In the film 101 Dalmatians it was the ideal choice for Cruella de Ville.*

mid-engined Panther 6, Panther's last model was the 1990 Solo, a monocoque aluminium-and-carbon-fibre 2+2 supercar fitted with Ford's Sierra Cosworth 2.0-litre turbo engine and Ferguson four-wheel drive, making it the world's first mid-engined four-wheel-drive production car. Some described it as the best handling road car of all time, but its disappointing performance, harsh ride and questionable build quality were unforgivable in a £40,000 ($67,000) sportscar. Even at that price, it was uneconomic to make. After one of the shortest production runs ever, the Solo was axed with just 12 cars sold.

In 1987 Panther had been acquired by the Korean firm SsangYong, which wound production down and used Panther expertise to design new SsangYong products. In retrospect, Panthers are often regarded as vulgar and unseemly jewellery, but they were all hand-built to the highest quality.

■ ABOVE LEFT *Most road testers were agreed that the Solo was an exquisite car to drive: very fast and extremely good around corners.*

■ ABOVE *The small small Kallista was Panther's car for the common man, and easily its best-selling model. It used Ford engines.*

■ LEFT *Mid-engined finesse from the 1990 Solo, a striking coupé with such advanced features as four-wheel drive, aluminium and carbonfibre bodywork and Cosworth turbo power.*

■ RIGHT *The Solo was a sad exit for Panther, who lost money on every example built. It remains extremely rare, since only 12 were sold.*

■ LEFT *Six wheels on my wagon. Only Panther could have come up with such an outlandish creation. Its mid-mounted turbocharged Cadillac V-eight was claimed to push this leviathan to 200mph (322kph).*

PANTHER LIMA (1976–82)	
Engine	4-cylinder
Capacity	2279cc
Power	108bhp @ 5000rpm
Transmission	4-speed manual 3-speed auto
Top speed	105mph (169kph)
No. built	918

PEUGEOT

■ PEUGEOT 205GTI

The Volkswagen Golf may have started the hot-hatch craze in the 1970s, but it was Peugeot that made the best of the breed in the 80s. Its 205GTI became a performance car legend, for it stood head-and-shoulders above the competition, right up until its death.

It started from a wonderful basis: the Pininfarina-designed 205 was a very competent little hatchback. Its combination of a pleasing shape, supple

■ RIGHT *No one who drove a 205GTI could fail to be impressed by its agility around corners.*

■ BELOW *The 205GTI sired the very special Turbo 16 mid-engined road/rally car. It arrived shortly before the Group B rally class was axed.*

ride and outstanding handling made it one of the most popular cars of its time – and it was still in production after 14 years. However, it cried out to have more power, and so the GTI was born in 1984.

Crisp, agile and offering more grip around corners than anyone had a right to expect from a car costing so little, the 205GTI was an instant hit.

Perhaps the power output of the first 1.6-litre engine was too low: 105bhp was less than rivals such as the Opel Astra GT/E and VW Golf GTI. Peugeot offered a Sport kit to boost power by 20bhp, but plainly the standard GTI needed to keep pace, and within two years Peugeot had upped the output of the 1.6-litre engine to 115bhp, and at the same time an even more powerful 130bhp 1.9-litre model was added. This larger engined version with its bigger alloy wheels proved to be the definitive GTI.

Inside, rally-style seats hugged the passengers and a tasteful arrangement of black, red and grey upholstery was standard. Instrumentation was complete and equipment generous. There wasn't much to criticize. The hard suspension gave an uncomfortable ride but this improved with successive tweaks. Build quality was a consistent problem, too, but probably the worst foible was on-the-limit handling. Although it took a lot to get a 205GTI out of shape around corners, when you did (by lifting off the throttle in mid-corner for instance), it was all rather a handful.

Another GTI variant was the 1986 CTI, the convertible version, which was partly built by Pininfarina. Most were made with 1.6-litre 115bhp engines, but eventually Peugeot succumbed and fitted the 130bhp 1.9 unit for another cracking car.

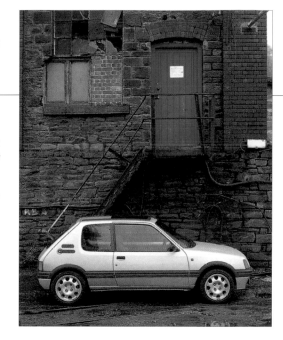

■ OPPOSITE *Compact, nimble, very grippy and entertainingly fast, the Peugeot 205GTI redefined the parameters of the hot hatch in the 1980s.*

When the 205GTI retired in 1994, there was no direct successor. The 306 was a much larger car, which, initially at least, had none of the GTI's performance and agility. Eventually, hot versions of the 306 and smaller 106 came along to fill the gap: the 306 S16 and GTi-6 were stormingly powerful hot hatches in the best traditions, while the 106GTI was possibly the most entertaining performance hatchback being made when it arrived in 1997.

By this stage, however, the heyday of the GTI had already passed. And in the 1980s, when it really was all the rage, the little Peugeot 205GTI was undoubtedly king of the breed.

■ LEFT *With the arrival of the 1.9-litre 205GTI (identifiable by its larger alloy wheels and 1.9 badging), power rose to 130bhp and the 205GTI stepped up another rung in the performance league.*

■ LEFT *Like the hatchback, Pininfarina designed the attractive CTI convertible, but here it also helped to manufacture it.*

■ BELOW *Top down, the CTI could be happily described as a 1980s equivalent of a sports roadster.*

PEUGEOT 205GTI (1984–94)	
Engine	4-cylinder
Capacity	1580–1905cc
Power	105–130bhp
Transmission	5-speed manual
Top speed	115–123mph (185–198kph)
No. built	Over 4 million 205s

■ RIGHT *Simple yet stylish, the GTI's interior was a feast of sporty details. The red/black/grey colour scheme was effective.*

PLYMOUTH

■ PLYMOUTH PROWLER

Having paved the way with the extraordinary Viper, Chrysler's management (headed by Bob Lutz) felt bullish enough to take its dream-car-to-production route one step further. The Plymouth Prowler was a rare example of a genuine show car reaching the public.

It all started with Tom Gale, the head of Chrysler's design team, who had always harboured a passion for hot rods.

the Prowler on the market. Its rod style was neat, melding classic themes such as separate fenders, jut-forward chin and a lack of spurious adornments with modern materials and a technological spin around the edges. Underpinning it all were massive 20in (50cm) rear wheels and fat 295-section rubber, alongside which the still-large 17in (43cm) front wheels looked dwarfed. There was no room for two spare wheels, so the rear ones had a run-flat capability. The sophisticated suspension was elegantly exposed to view. Cockpit space was generous, although the boot (trunk) was completely taken up by the folding roof when it was down.

He penned a modern interpretation of the classic "bucket-rod" theme and put it on Chrysler's stand at the 1993 Detroit Auto Show. The reaction to it was so positive that Chrysler's board ordered a feasibility study and gave it the green light for production with a budget of $75 million – peanuts in Detroit terms.

Chrysler's theory was that hot rods were ingrained in the American subconscious and lots of people actually wanted to own one but never had the time or inclination to build their own. Step in the Plymouth Prowler, ready-made in Detroit for such an audience.

There was nothing else remotely like

■ LEFT *The styling themes were all pure American hot rod, with a dash of modern spice to give it a marketing shine. Only 3,000 were to be made in the first year.*

■ ABOVE *Hot-rod fans might have been disappointed by the fitment of a V-six engine rather than a V-eight, but in truth it was quick enough for most tastes.*

In construction the Prowler was formed of steel and aluminium panels over a steel frame. Despite its radical looks, it complied with US safety laws, which necessitated such features as big front and rear bumpers and a high-level stop light.

Hot-rod fans were mildly miffed when, instead of a true blue American V-eight engine, Chrysler decided to fit its Vision 3.5-litre V-six instead. Still, with its 218bhp it was more than fast enough to satisfy most tastes: since it weighed only 1315kg (2900lb), 0–60mph (0–96kph) came in an impressive 7.7 seconds, and top speed – limited by poor aerodynamics – was 125mph (200kph).

Chrysler showed the series-form Prowler at the 1996 Detroit show, and production was due to begin for the 1998 model year. All 3000 of the first year's production were to be painted the same colour – purple! If nothing else, the Prowler raised dowdy Plymouth's profile. By tapping into a national passion for hot-rodding, Plymouth had cleverly earned itself a whole set of values that no amount of advertising could ever have created.

PLYMOUTH PROWLER (1997–)	
Engine	V-six cylinder
Capacity	3523cc
Power	218bhp @ 5850rpm
Transmission	4-speed automatic
Top speed	125mph (200kph)
No. built	Still in production

■ ABOVE *The chiselled jaw and narrow grille were genuine hot-rod throwbacks, although the "dodgem" bumpers were a concession to current safety laws.*

■ LEFT *If you went out on the prowl, the original Plymouth show car featured this natty trailer for your effects.*

PONTIAC

■ PONTIAC FIREBIRD

The first-generation Pontiac Firebird was sired by Chevrolet's Camaro, arriving some six months after it, and differing only in terms of trim, engine choices and the traditional Pontiac split-grille treatment of its nasal styling. It was restyled below the waist for 1969 and given a dose of safety equipment, while convertible versions were also listed.

The most classic of the early Firebirds was the 1969 Trans Am. It took its name from the Trans-American road-race series organized by the Sports Car Club of America, and began a whole dynasty of Firebirds with this name. Its special white-and-blue stripes paintwork, rear spoiler, beefed-up chassis and 335–345bhp Ram Air power made it distinctive and much better on the tarmac than standard Firebirds.

An all-new Firebird arrived as a mid-1970 model with a distinctive style that lasted through 1981, minor restyles occurring for 1974, 1977 and 1979. Again there was a high-performance

■ LEFT *This is where the Firebird story first began: a sister model to the Chevrolet Camaro with a traditional Pontiac split-grille nose.*

Trans Am model, which was a highly marginal seller to start with (only 2116 sales in 1971), but became the most popular Firebird of all by the end of the decade (more than 93,000 were sold in 1978). There were also standard, luxury Esprit and Formula models.

The Firebird almost died in 1972 when General Motors began asking serious questions about the future of the performance-car market. Luckily it was decided to keep it going and the

PONTIAC FIREBIRD (1971–81)	
Engine	6-/V-six/V-eight-cylinder
Capacity	3785–7456cc
Power	105–345bhp
Transmission	4-speed auto 5-speed manual
Top speed	96–125mph (154–201kph)
No. built	1,061,719

■ LEFT *There was no mistaking the snout of the second-generation Firebird. This is a 1972 Trans Am, the high-performance model of the range.*

■ ABOVE *The 1974 Firebird was restyled with Federal laws in mind. The car pictured is a Trans Am 455 Super Duty.*

■ ABOVE *Towards the end of its life, the second-generation Firebird sprouted decoration (as this 1980 Trans Am shows) but lost power.*

■ ABOVE *The third-generation Firebird series arrived in 1982. This is a line-up from 1987, when the 5.7 litre V-eight reappeared.*

■ LEFT *The Trans Am name-plate continued to denote the top-of-the-range performance version.*

Firebird did extremely well for GM.

Power dropped steadily through the 1970s due to increasingly strict US government emission controls. Still, the Firebird never succumbed to pressure to lose its optional V-eight power, and a turbocharged 301 cubic inch (4936 cubic centimetre) version added a bit of spice for the 1980 model year.

For the third-generation, 1982 Firebird, again the basic bodywork was shared with Chevrolet's Camaro, but Pontiac stylists designed a distinctive chiselled, cowled-headlamp nose for the 'Bird. Base, S/E and Trans Am models were listed, while a return to the big 350 cubic inch (5740 cubic centimetre) V-eight arrived for 1987, also powering a top-level model called the GTA with

its distinctive spoiler and skirts. With 245bhp in its most powerful guise, the Firebird could manage 0–60mph (0–96kph) in just 5.4 seconds.

Falling sales and a lack-lustre image in the face of ever-improving imported competition characterized the final years of this long-running design. It was not

finally replaced until 1993, when the latest Firebird was unveiled (again closely based on the new Chevy Camaro but featuring a sharp, eagle-like nose, which varied slightly according to model). Initially available only as a coupé, an attractive-looking full convertible was added in 1994.

■ ABOVE *Quintessentially American, the Firebird (seen here in Trans Am guise) offered coupé style and V-eight power for a bargain price.*

■ ABOVE *This is a 1991 Firebird GTA. Two years later the series was replaced by a new fourth-generation Firebird.*

P O R S C H E

■ BELOW *Although it was first launched in 1963, essentially the same 911 design was still being produced in 1979.*

■ PORSCHE 911

Today's Porsche 911 shares only a few nuts and bolts with the original edition of 1963, yet few modern classics have such a strong hereditary line and identity. The original Porsche 911 was to have been called the 901 until Peugeot reminded Porsche that it had the copyright on all model numbers with "01" in them, and so the magical formula was born.

Styled by Ferry Porsche's eldest son Butzi, it is still recognizable today, although spoilers and fat arches altered its elegant profile throughout the 1970s. The development potential of the flat-six engine, with one of the most distinctive growling engine notes on the road, seems

■ LEFT *When Porsche launched a convertible version of the 911, it became instantly popular. This is a Carrera Cabriolet.*

■ BELOW *Porsche brought turbocharging into the modern age. Its 911 Turbo was a hugely powerful supercar, easily the fastest-accelerating production car of its day.*

limitless: it grew from just 2.0 litres to 3.6 litres in the latest versions, while power leapt fom 125bhp to 408bhp in the latest Turbo – leaving aside the 450bhp of the 911-based 959.

For drivers, the best of the "classic" 911 bunch was the 2.7 RS Carrera of the 1970s, a lightweight homologation special with stiffer suspension and a hallmark duck-tail spoiler. There have been some surprisingly mild variants, too, such as the Sportomatic with its semi-auto clutchless gear-shift and the 912, a budget model using the four-cylinder engine of the old 356.

Tail-happy handling has always been part of the 911's mystique, but much of that was cured early on when the wheelbase was lengthened. For modern 911 owners, talk of "lift-off (trailing-throttle) oversteer" is largely bar-room bravado. In any case, for those who harboured serious doubts about the handling, in the 1990s Porsche offered a four-wheel-drive model called the Carrera 4. More to the point was the car's superb steering and progressive, powerful brakes, which gave the driver such vivid road-feel.

Those who get hooked on the 911 rarely go back to other cars. The legends about build quality and reliability are all true, and longevity is another strong suit since all 911s have been built out of non-rusting galvanized steel since the mid-70s. The 911 image has changed over the years though: for the buyer of the 60s and 70s, the 911 was the choice of the seasoned connoisseur; by the mid-80s it had become a yuppie icon, a rolling symbol of fast, flash cash. For some, including Porsche, this image has lingered a little too long.

The Porsche 911 is an abiding legend

■ ABOVE *The characteristic whale-tail rear spoiler of the Turbo found its way on to most versions of the 911 during the 1980s.*

■ RIGHT *Oversteer was always part of the 911 mystique, although the limits of its roadholding were always very high up the scale.*

that has defied all attempts at replacing it. By rights it should have been killed off by the 928 in the mid-70s but somehow sales never slackened off: the worthy but uncharismatic 928 had none of the 911's enduring appeal and Porsche has no plans to do away with its classic rear-engined coupé. After all, it has been the company's meal ticket through some tough times. In 1997 the 911 was replaced by an all-new flat-six-engined coupé with water-cooling. The name? 911...

PORSCHE 911 (1963–)	
Engine	6-cylinder
Capacity	1991–3600cc
Power	125–408bhp
Transmission	4/5/6-speed manual semi-auto
Top speed	130–183mph (209–294kph)
No. built	Approx. 430,000 (to date)

■ LEFT *Porsche introduced a four-wheel-drive system in the Carrera 4 in 1989 for sure-footed handling. Note how far behind the rear axle the six-cylinder engine is.*

■ ABOVE *The 911 evolved through several incarnations. This is a Carrera RS model, a stripped-out version with a 260bhp version of the classic flat-six engine.*

PORSCHE

■ PORSCHE 928

The whole of Porsche's glowing reputation was based on a format that it had used since 1948, namely a rear-mounted engine. The 924 of 1975 was its first-ever front-engined car but, since this was an Audi cast-off, it is fair to say that the 928 was the first car conceived by the Porsche team to have a front engine.

The 928 was always intended as a range-topping supercar, but secretly Porsche hoped it would prove to be a natural successor to the rear-engined 911. In the end, of course, it never did displace its more sporting sibling, and the 911 remained the seminal Porsche. In truth, the 928's main success was in attracting a new class of buyer to the Porsche brand, someone who might otherwise have elected to buy a Mercedes SLC or Jaguar XJS, for this was more of a grand tourer than an outright sportscar.

Porsche built an all-new 4.5-litre V-eight for the 928, which was fabulously

■ ABOVE *The flop-forward headlamps and highly rounded styling of the 928 met with some controversy.*

■ ABOVE *The wrap-around facia gave the impression of completely cosseting the driver. The standard of finish and level of luxury were of a very high order.*

■ ABOVE *Porsche originally harboured ideas that the 928 might one day replace the long-lived 911, but instead it slotted in as a top-of-range grand tourer.*

PORSCHE 928 (1977–95)	
Engine	V-eight-cylinder
Capacity	4474–5399cc
Power	240–350bhp
Transmission	5-speed manual 4-speed automatic
Top speed	143–171mph (230–275kph)
No. built	Approx. 35,000

■ LEFT *The GTS was a run-out (final) version, and the pinnacle of a long line of 928s.*

smooth and flexible but ultimately not as quick as the 911. There was a choice of rear-mounted manual transmission or, more commonly, Mercedes-built automatic. An attempt to give it some more power was made with the later 4.7-litre 928S (which had an extra 60bhp at 300bhp).

In character, the 928 was ruthlessly efficient rather than exciting, a trait that its clean but uninvolving styling seemed to exacerbate. It was also very comfortable, at least for the two front passengers; rear seat space was available, but very limited. Lavish equipment levels matched its "soft" image. Handling could not be faulted, and it was as forgiving as the 911 was tricky at its limit.

■ ABOVE *The front-mounted V-eight engine gave the 928 a very different character from more traditional Porsche models: powerful yet unruffled and refined.*

■ BELOW *In its ultimate guise, Porsche tried to give the 928 more sporting appeal, with fatter wheels, lower suspension and lower-profile tyres.*

■ ABOVE *With its 5.4-litre 350bhp engine, the GTS was the fastest and most rewarding of all 928 models, but always a real rarity.*

Power jumped again in 1986 with the launch of the S4. Its 5.0-litre power-plant now had a twin-cam head, 32 valves and a maximum output of 320bhp: the 928 was finally coming of age. The S4 restyle altered the nose and tail sections.

The best versions of all were saved for last, however. To counter criticisms that

this was not as sporting as some rivals, Porsche offered a GT version with an extra 10bhp, electronic limited slip differential and sports suspension (which improved handling but made the ride harder). The package became even sharper with the 1992 GTS, now sporting a 5.4-litre 350bhp engine, wider wheels and a more vigorous feel.

After a production run of 18 years, the 928 was retired in 1995. The model was not as successful as Porsche had initially hoped, but it had provided a useful lesson: traditional Porsche people stuck with what they knew and liked – the 911 – and the Stuttgart firm meddled with this fact of life at its peril. It has never looked back.

PORSCHE

■ PORSCHE 924/944

The Porsche 924 was conceived in the early 1970s as a joint project with Volkswagen/Audi, to be designed by Porsche but produced and marketed by Volkswagen using as many stock VW parts as possible. The engine was the fuel-injected 2.0-litre unit from the Audi 100 – also found in the VW LT van – and, while the rear transaxle was new, the gears inside were Audi, too.

It was only when the fuel crisis began to bite hard, and sales of the ugly-

■ BELOW *In Carrera form (a 1980 limited edition), the 924 was very powerful and boasted a dramatic body kit that presaged the 944.*

■ ABOVE *In profile, the 944 was very similar to the 924, but its flared wheel-arches were an instant give-away that this had pukka Porsche power.*

duckling VW-Porsche 914 began to flag, that Porsche realized it was faced with the prospect of having no cheap sports-car to sell in the second half of the 70s. With the 911's future also uncertain, Porsche decided to take over the project as a pure Porsche model, with production subcontracted to VW.

Launched in 1975, the 924 was an instant success. However, this was no 911: the van-derived engine could be raucous when pressed, even if it endowed the 924 with brisk acceleration and a 125mph (201kph) top speed in its long-legged fifth gear. More impressive was the handling, the perfect 50/50 weight distribution giving the 924 a well-balanced poise that allowed even novices to drive quickly and safely, with

PORSCHE 924/944 (1975–93)	
Engine	4-cylinder
Capacity	1984–2990cc
Power	125–211bhp
Transmission	4/5-speed manual 3-speed auto
Top speed	125–160mph (201–257kph)
No. built	122,304/163,820

■ RIGHT *Many people were surprised to find Porsche producing a front-engined four-cylinder car, and indeed the 924 began life as an Audi project.*

■ RIGHT *This is a full line-up of 944 models at Porsche's Stuttgart facility.*

precise, informative and light steering – not unlike a 911's – allied to slight roll angles. The gearbox was pleasant to use and a few 924s were even built with automatic transmission.

The 924 Turbo of 1978 hardened the model's performance image in the late 70s. Its 170bhp came courtesy of a KKK turbocharger. Top speed surged from 125mph (201kph) to 141mph (227kph), and acceleration was almost in the supercar class with 0–60mph (0–96kph) in 6.9 seconds. Stiffer suspension and better brakes meant the handling was even more polished. Cooling slots in the nose and discreet spoilers singled this model out from the the ordinary 924.

In the 1980s, the 944, with a proper Porsche 2.5-litre four-cylinder engine – effectively half a 928 V-eight – finally shook off associations with the VW LT van, although the 924 itself lingered on until 1985. In fact, the 944 was a very different car with big wheel-arches, fatter wheels and tyres and a lower stance. It got twin cams in 1986, and was joined by a Turbo version in 1986, that was good for nearly 160mph (257kph). The last-of-the-line three-litre models came in both closed and convertible forms. Even then the model did not die: the 1993 Porsche 968, which lasted until 1995, was a radically evolved version of the 944.

■ LEFT *The 944 was undoubtedly one of the best-handling cars made in the 1980s, thanks to its wide stance and competent chassis engineering.*

■ LEFT *Even the basic 944S was a quick car, but in Turbo form the 944 was good for 160mph (257kph).*

■ BELOW *In many ways, the 944 Cabriolet was the most attractive 944 variant. Its hood (top) was simple and effective.*

■ RIGHT *The final evolution of the 924/944 series was the 968 of 1993–5, sold in coupé and convertible styles.*

PORSCHE

■ PORSCHE 959

Porsche built the 959 with the intention that it should become a formidable Group B racing car, and it was shown at the 1983 Frankfurt Motor Show as the "Gruppe B". But when Group B cars were banned from racing in 1986, Porsche switched the emphasis of its design programme to create the ultimate road car.

It started by drastically reshaping the basic 911 body, using high-tech plastics and aluminium doors and front lid. The suspension was all new and multi-adjustable, while a clever system monitored tyre pressures on the move.

Then there was the engine, a monstrous twin turbocharged version of the familiar flat six. With only 2.85 litres, it developed 450bhp and could accelerate the 1450kg (3200lb) 959 from rest to 60mph (96kph) in an unbelievable 3.6 seconds, or 0–100mph (0–161kph) in a stunning 8.2 seconds.

The *pièce de résistance* was undoubtedly the transmission. Not only was four-wheel drive permanent, and not only did it have six speeds, but there

was also a choice of four computer-controlled traction settings to suit different conditions: thick snow/mud, ice, wet and dry. Even so, the rear-engined 959 was challenging to drive.

Only existing Porsche owners could buy the £155,000 ($261,000) car, and very quickly a "grey market" sprang up, boosting used prices to ridiculous levels. Since less than 300 were ever made, demand would always outstrip supply, and remaining examples are blue-chip classics of the first order.

■ ABOVE *The idea for the 959 was born as early as 1983 when this so-called Gruppe B prototype was displayed at the Frankfurt Motor Show.*

■ LEFT *The 959 sat low and squat on multi-adjustable suspension. It also had permanent (full-time) four-wheel drive, six speeds and selectable traction control.*

PORSCHE 959 (1987–88)	
Engine	6-cylinder
Capacity	2850cc
Power	450bhp @ 6500rpm
Transmission	6-speed manual
Top speed	197mph (315kph)
No. built	283

■ BELOW *Wild in every way, the 959 was loosely based on the 911, but its bodywork was drastically altered, featuring both plastic and aluminium body panels.*

■ ABOVE *Tremendous urge was tempered by phenomenal grip. Even so, driving a 959 was never a relaxing experience, thanks to the explosive power of 450 horses sitting in the tail.*

◼ PORSCHE BOXSTER

After the death of Porsche's front-engined models (the 968 and 928), the Stuttgart firm was left with just one model once again, the venerable rear-engined 911. Having passed through such a painful period of front-engined cars, Porsche elected to take a new direction with its first all-new model in 18 years: the Boxster.

What distinguished the new Boxster was its engine position – in the middle of the car, driving the rear wheels. Porsche claimed that "the mid-engine provides ideal driving dynamics", and the world was forced to agree.

The new Boxster was fabulously entertaining to drive, balanced, responsive and surprisingly forgiving. Powered by a brand new 204bhp 2.5-litre six-cylinder "boxer" engine, in the best Porsche tradition, the Boxster was

as fast as it was smooth. Porsche claimed a top speed of 149mph (240kph) and a 0–62mph (0–100kph) time of 6.9 seconds, or slightly less if you ordered the attractive option of the Tiptronic S gearbox, which allowed gear-changes to be made from paddle controls on the steering wheel.

The four-piston mono-block brake caliper system was for the first time fitted to a road-going Porsche, and was claimed to have 100 per cent fade-free characteristics. It enabled the Boxster to pull up short from 62mph (100kph) in just 2.7 seconds.

Perhaps the Boxster's greatest allure

lay in its purposeful styling. Boasting the lowest drag coefficient of any car in its class (0.31), it was elegant, smooth and timeless. The striking headlamps were shrouded by durable plastic covers.

An enticing cockpit boasted instruments grouped in an arc, slightly overlapping each other. The electric soft-top could be lowered in just 12 seconds and stowed underneath a metal cover.

The Boxster undoubtedly represented a serious part of Porsche's future. Priced very competitively to do battle with the Mercedes-Benz SLK and BMW Z3, it also attracted a whole new generation of drivers to the Porsche marque.

◼ LEFT *From within the engagingly styled interior, the electric soft-top could be folded down in just 20 seconds.*

◼ ABOVE *Beautifully balanced in action thanks to its mid-engined layout, the Boxster was reasonably fast and boasted race-car braking ability.*

◼ LEFT *The name Boxster was a joining of two Porsche classics, the "boxer" engine layout and the Speedster body style.*

◼ BELOW *There was little room for doubt that Porsche created one of the most desirable of all sportscars in the Boxster, and yet this was its entry-level model.*

PORSCHE BOXSTER (1996–)	
Engine	6-cylinder
Capacity	2480cc
Power	204bhp @ 6000rpm
Transmission	5-speed manual
Top speed	149mph (240kph)
No. built	Still in production

RENAULT

RENAULT 5 TURBO

The idea of a car created specially to compete in rallies was Renault's. The 5 Turbo, introduced in 1978, spawned a string of copycat homologation specials like the Lancia S4 and Ford RS200, all sold for road use as well, because the rules stated that a minimum number had to be built. As a pioneer, the Renault was also the only rally car which made complete sense as a road car.

In fact, an impressive tally of nearly 5,000 Renault 5 Turbos were built because of customer demand. It's easy to appreciate why. The 5 Turbo had a centrally mounted turbo intercooled engine, which offered scorching acceleration, massive grip and endless handling entertainment.

Very little of the shopping (standard) Renault 5 (Le Car in the US) remained. Renault's Alpine factory bolted on

■ LEFT *The 5 Turbo launched the rally-spec homologation generation. In style and driving character it was a wild experience.*

■ ABOVE *The mid-engine looks tiny – in fact, it was only 1.4 litres – but it kicked out 160bhp for some screaming acceleration.*

■ ABOVE *Unlike the Gallic artscape of the Turbo 1, the Turbo 2's interior was based on that of the standard Renault 5 (Le Car).*

wildly flared wheel-arches, gaping cooling vents and big spoilers, and the doors, roof and tailgate of the first cars were in aluminium. The interior was a typically French mix of bold primary colours and avant-garde design.

Mechanically, the story was even more divergent. Racing suspension, big brakes and hugely fat tyres

complemented the heavily heat-shielded engine (which sat just inches from your ears, inside the cockpit).

From 1983, there was a Turbo 2 version with minor trim changes, a recognizably Renault 5-derived interior and a heavier all-steel body; in contrast to the first edition (of which 1,830 were built), some 3,167 Turbo 2s were sold.

■ ABOVE *In the massively flared arches sat very wide alloy wheels and tyres, which boasted huge grip.*

RENAULT 5 TURBO (1978–86)	
Engine	4-cylinder
Capacity	1397cc
Power	160bhp @ 6000rpm
Transmission	5-speed manual
Top speed	125mph (201kph)
No. built	4,997

■ LEFT *Although its name and some body panels were derived from the Renault 5 shopping car, the 5 Turbo was a real mid-engined beast.*

■ RIGHT *The 1984–91 GTA was the latest in a long line of Renault-based sportscars from Alpine, which was France's equivalent of Porsche.*

■ RENAULT ALPINE GTA/A610

Launched in 1984, the Renault Alpine GTA was the last of a famous line of rear-engined French sportscars using Renault V-six power in a steel back-bone chassis. Gunning for the Porsche 911 market, it offered superb driver involvement and high levels of grip (despite the tail-happy layout) but never managed to tempt many buyers away from Porsche.

They were certainly quick cars, particularly in Turbo form, topping 150mph (241kph) and turning in 0–60mph (0–96kph) times in the six-second bracket. Drivers loved the GTA for its feel and responsiveness, yet it was a comfortable, quiet long-distance machine. Despite its exotic looks, it was surprisingly practical, with usable rear seats and rust-free plastic bodywork. The Douvrin V-six engine – straight out of the big Renault 25 – offered no reliability problems either, and the overall quality of the cars was acceptable, if not in the 911's league.

In 1991, the GTA evolved to become the A610 with a few styling tweaks that somehow robbed the crisp-edged shape of character but gave it broader showroom appeal: pop-headlights are the quickest way of identifying the new model. The power of the Turbo model was hiked up to 250bhp thanks to a

■ ABOVE *The unusually styled interior raided the Renault parts bin for its switchgear.*

larger 3.0-litre engine, and top speed rose to 165mph (265kph) with no turbo-lag. The double-wishbone suspension was tweaked to cure any hint of twitchyness suffered by the older model. With the inclusion of power-steering, parking the A610 wasn't such a muscle-building exercise either.

The GTA and A610 Alpines were hailed as classics while still in production, but always lived in the shade of the Porsche 911. Production ended in 1995, with no successor.

RENAULT ALPINE GTA/A610 (1984–95)	
Engine	V-six-cylinder
Capacity	2458–2975cc
Power	160–250bhp
Transmission	5-speed manual
Top speed	146–165mph (235–265kph)
No. built	17,450

■ ABOVE *An expanded 3.0-litre V-six engine sat in the tail. It had 250bhp on tap.*

■ LEFT *In Turbo form the GTA was exceptionally fast. The rear-sited V-six engine inevitably caused tail-happy manners, but the GTA was grippy nonetheless.*

■ RIGHT *The A610 Turbo stepped up a rung: a 160mph (257kph) top speed and improved handling made it a Porsche rival.*

RENAULT

■ RENAULT ESPACE

Other car manufacturers can lay claim to having invented the people carrier, otherwise known as the Multi Purpose Vehicle (MPV), but Renault was the first to produce an MPV specifically created from the ground up as such and make it popular. It revolutionized the car market and the repercussions of its success are still being felt, with every major manufacturer producing a rival.

The origins of the Espace actually began with the French sportscar constructor and aerospace leader Matra. In the late 1970s, it was allied to Simca-Talbot and produced a proposal based on the Horizon for a radical "one-box" people carrier. But Matra was sold on to Renault and with it went the MPV project. Renault immediately recognized

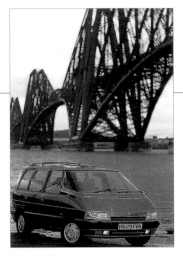

■ ABOVE *With a restyle in 1991, the Espace moved on to ever-greater success.*

its potential and brought its new Espace to production in 1984, the same year as Chrysler Corporation's minivans.

The first and most striking feature was the shape, an exceptionally neat and integrated design with a long, steeply raked windscreen. In construction it was equally different: a steel-skeleton frame clothed with plastic panels.

The single most significant factor in the Espace equation was its interior. The fact that it was spacious, airy and cleanly designed was secondary to its tremendous adaptability. There were three rows of seats for up to seven passengers in all, and each of these seats could be removed to increase luggage space. The front seats could

■ ABOVE *Tremendous adaptability was the Espace's strength: the front seats could swivel around, and you could fold down a central seat to make a picnic table.*

swivel round to face the others, and the central one could fold to make a table. Picnic-goers and mobile office workers were happy and Renault never looked back, dominating the European MPV market with successive Espace cars.

■ ABOVE *Up to seven seats could be fitted in the Espace, and then removed individually at will to turn it into a load-lugger.*

RENAULT ESPACE (1984–91)	
Engine	4-cylinder
Capacity	1995cc
Power	103–120bhp
Transmission	5-speed
Top speed	106–111mph (171–179kph)
No. built	147,960

■ LEFT *Renault inherited the innovative Espace project from Matra, and made it Europe's first – and the world's most convincing – MPV or people carrier.*

■ RIGHT *The van-like driving position was criticized but it gave wonderful visibility.*

■ RENAULT TWINGO

One of the first things that Renault's new design chief Patrick Le Quément did when he joined the firm was to let it be known that Renault would be taking the lead in design terms, producing the best innovative new cars. The Twingo was the perfect expression of this ideal.

Le Quément skilfully extended the idea of the "one-box" design pioneered by Renault's Espace to the smallest car in the range. The line from the front bumper to the top of the windscreen was one elegant curve, broken only by the characterful hooded headlamps and bonnet (hood) cooling vents.

The hatchback Twingo may have looked cute from the outside but its cabin was its best feature. The digital instruments were sited in a pod in the centre of the dash, and all the switchgear was in contrasting colours and a tactile material. There was a huge amount of space, made all the more practical by the four individually reclining and sliding seats. Optional extras included a full sliding sunroof and air-conditioning.

Considering the avant-garde look of the Twingo, it was mildly disappointing to find old-world mechanicals underneath, taken directly from the antiquated Renault 5. The engine was harsh and the

■ LEFT *The Espace-style "monobox" design was applied to a miniature city car to create the brilliant Twingo.*

■ ABOVE *Little eyebrows over the headlamps and interesting air vents in the bonnet (hood) added character to the design.*

■ ABOVE *The Twingo was the ideal city car: very compact, nimble and economical.*

road behaviour nothing special. It took until 1996 for Renault to fit a modern engine in the form of a brand-new 1149cc unit with more power and extra zing. An automatic version dubbed Easy was launched at the same time.

The Twingo rose to become the best-selling car in France as buyers rushed to share in its chic, and a whole culture seemed to spring up around it. The millionth example was built in 1997.

RENAULT TWINGO (1992–)	
Engine	4-cylinder
Capacity	1149–1239cc
Power	54–58bhp
Transmission	5-speed manual 3-speed automatic
Top speed	93mph (150kph)
No. built	Still in production

■ RIGHT *Très jolie – the Twingo endeared itself to French buyers, who elevated it to the Number One best-seller in 1995.*

■ FAR RIGHT *Interior packaging was impressive, and the rear seats could slide fore-and-aft individually. Note the centrally mounted digital dash.*

RENAULT

■ RENAULT SPORT SPIDER

So-called niche cars began to assume tremendous importance in the 1990s. Sales of mainstream models went down while low-production models sold proportionately more. Usually, niche cars were merely cleverly positioned conventional designs, but that is not a description you could apply to Renault's amazing Sport Spider.

The recipe was exciting, and wildly out of the ordinary for a major company like Renault. Here was a car built for one purpose only: pure driving enjoyment. The brief called for a lightweight, mid-engined sports two-seater, which was so pure in its ethos that it made do without a roof.

Indeed, the first Sport Spider made do without even a windscreen. The design team, led by the brilliant Patrick Le Quément, sculpted a radical shape, which incorporated a solid wind deflector where a windscreen might have been. Later on, a version was offered with a windscreen and wiper in

■ ABOVE *Renault was amazingly ambitious and adventurous with its Sport Spider: mid-engined, roofless and even devoid of a windscreen!*

■ BELOW *The styling was by Patrick Le Quément's innovative team at Renault. Although a return to the theme of the Lotus 7, it was unashamedly modern in appearance.*

■ ABOVE *A deliberately sparse cabin reflected the lightweight, bare-boned nature of this stripped-out road racer. Note the exposed aluminium basis (framework).*

place, but you still got no side windows or roof. That didn't seem to matter, because owners got the chance to drive and enjoy a car which had the look and feel of an advanced concept car.

The Sport Spider was equally radical in construction. The chassis was made of lightweight aluminium, which was also extremely rigid. The suspension was by race-inspired, rose (spherical)-jointed double wishbones, and the huge vented disc brakes came from the A610 supercar.

For its power, Renault opted to fit the sizzling 150bhp two-litre engine of the Clio Williams. That was sufficient to take it to 62mph (100kph) from rest in just 6.9 seconds.

■ RIGHT *The Sport Spider was also meant for racing, and Renault organized a one-make series, which supported British Touring Car races in 1996.*

Overall the Sport Spider was incredibly quick, both in a straight line and through corners. At 1740lb (790kg), it may not have been as light as a Lotus Elise, but it was certainly no heavyweight. It cornered with almost no roll.

The umbrella organization that created this unique car, Renault Sport, also ran a racing series exclusively for the Sport Spider. Race cars got more power (175bhp), so the action was fast, furious and incredibly exciting, and attracted many talented drivers and large viewing audiences.

This was perhaps the main point of the project. Renault knew the Sport Spider was not going to be a strong seller. It cost much more than rivals like the Lotus Elise and Caterham 21, and it was obviously too impractical to be used on a daily basis. Production volumes (at Renault's Alpine works in Dieppe) were tiny but the publicity gained for Renault's radical design work was huge – and its courage in putting such a machine into production at all was widely applauded.

■ ABOVE *In practice, most Sport Spider customers opted for the version with the full windscreen.*

RENAULT SPORT SPIDER (1995–)	
Engine	4-cylinder
Capacity	1998cc
Power	150bhp
Transmission	5-speed manual
Top speed	134mph (216kph)
No. built	Still in production

■ RIGHT *This image suggests that the Sport Spider was somehow acceptable in rain. True, you had a windscreen wiper on this version, but no roof or side windows.*

ROLLS-ROYCE

ROLLS-ROYCE CAMARGUE

The Pininfarina-styled Rolls-Royce Camargue, Crewe's flamboyant 1970s super-coupé, was a car for kings, princes, diplomats and superstars, a hedonistic two-door with no true rival. There was little to match it for size in the coupé stakes, and nothing approaching its price: the Camargue was the most expensive car on the market at its launch in 1975, 50 per cent dearer than a Corniche convertible.

Pininfarina was the natural choice for styling this new flagship, having done one-off designs on various Bentleys and Rolls-Royces in the 50s. Sergio Pininfarina even moderated his usual fee, but the styling got a luke-warm reception from some quarters. Farina did the interior, too, and designed a new dashboard using standard Silver Shadow instruments but with square black plates similar to an aircraft cockpit.

Launched in Sicily in 1975, the 120mph (193kph) Camargue was the first Rolls-Royce to have curved window glass and the first ever designed to metric dimensions. Mechanically, the car used a slightly more powerful 6.75-litre alloy Rolls pushrod V-eight engine and the usual independent suspension and complex hydraulic systems for the four-wheel disc brakes and self-levelling suspension.

■ BELOW *The Camargue was one of Rolls-Royce's most exclusive models. Over an 11-year period, only just over 500 were made.*

■ ABOVE *If you wanted the most expensive car in the world in 1975, the Rolls-Royce Camargue was your choice: a two-door coupé from the "best car company in the world".*

The star technical attraction of the £29,000 ($48,850) Camargue was its superb split-level air-conditioning system, which cost as much as a Mini and had the cooling capacity of 30 domestic refrigerators.

Each Camargue took six months to make, at a rate never higher than one per week. Unsurprisingly, the Camargue's best market was the USA (280 cars); 75 went to Saudi Arabia, while in Europe the car's best market was its native Britain with 136 sold.

■ ABOVE *Pininfarina also styled the interior, which was a palace of leather and wood, topped off by the most sophisticated air-conditioning system yet seen in a car.*

■ ABOVE *The clean and simple styling was done by Pininfarina, and was good enough to hide the model's considerable bulk.*

■ ABOVE *Fit and finish were superlative, while the detailing was quintessentially British, with hand-stitching and chrome handles.*

ROLLS-ROYCE CAMARGUE (1975–86)	
Engine	V-eight-cylinder
Capacity	6750cc
Power	Not quoted
Top speed	120mph (193kph)
No. built	534

ROVER

■ ROVER SD1

With the P6 saloon (sedan) car range
Rover had scored an undoubted winner,
as European journalists recognized
when they awarded it the very first Car
of the Year award. Its successor, the so-
called SD1, won it again in 1977.

For a Rover, the new SD1 3500 was
pretty radical. Gone were all traces of
chrome and all wood dashboards, which
were seemingly permanent fixtures on
Rover's past. Gone was the traditional,
sober saloon layout in favour of a
hatchback. And the interior (with its
separate "box of instruments") was
anything but conservative.

The architect of the SD1 shape was
Rover's David Bache, and he had the
probity to acknowledge the Ferrari
Daytona as a direct influence: the

prominent mid-riff indentation and
narrow headlamps were unmistakable.
As a result, the 3500 looked distinctly
sleek for 1976.

As launched, the 3500 had Rover's
familiar V-eight engine. In other
respects it was a mixture of old and new:
the live rear axle and drum brakes were
hardly ground-breaking, but the
MacPherson strut front suspension
sharpened up the handling considerably.
Less powerful 2000, 2300 and

2600 six cylinder versions followed.

The best model of all was the 1982
Vitesse with its 190bhp fuel-injection
engine, lowered suspension, spoked
alloy wheels and tailgate spoiler.
Although it was rare (less than 4,000
were built), the Vitesse added a true
performance edge to the SD1 range,
which was replaced in 1986.

■ LEFT *Rover's David
Bache admitted to
using Ferrari's
Daytona as
inspiration. For a
luxury saloon
(sedan), the SD1
looked extremely
sporty.*

■ ABOVE *The most powerful SD1 model of all was the
Vitesse, with its 190bhp fuel-injected V-eight, lowered
suspension and tailgate spoiler.*

■ ABOVE *Rover departed from its traditions
with the interior. Most notable was the
separate binnacle housing all the instruments.*

■ ABOVE *The range
of SD1 engines
started with a 2.0-
litre four-cylinder
unit and went up
to the popular
3.5-litre V-eight.*

■ LEFT *The ultra-
quick Vitesse was a
fitting end to an
innovative chapter
in Rover's
long history.*

ROVER SD1 3500 (1976–86)	
Engine	V-eight-cylinder
Capacity	3528cc
Power	155–190bhp
Transmission	5-speed manual 3-speed automatic
Top speed	125–135mph (201–217kph)
No. built	113,966

SAAB

■ SAAB 99 TURBO

Sweden's aerospace leaders are very well known for their motor cars, and the string of models Saab has produced for over 50 years have always been unconventional, highly distinctive and instantly recognizable. The 99 Turbo was a model that launched Saab into a new era.

Saab's traditional front-wheel-drive layout remained, but the engine was new, jointly developed by Triumph and Saab. When it came to extracting more performance from this engine, Saab adopted turbocharging technology. Turbos were still a novelty in 1977, and Saab made the turbocharger an art-form of its very own. Long after other makers had abandoned this route, Saab plugged away with it as a performance and emissions device.

As a result of turbocharging, the standard fuel-injected 2.0-litre engine's power was boosted from 118bhp to 145bhp, very high for an engine of this size in 1977. New heights of performance were achieved – 0–60mph (0–96kph) in nine seconds, 125mph (201kph) top speed – though Saab never did iron out drastic turbo lag (the time it took for the turbo to cut in once the throttle had been pressed), nor a tendency to ferocious take-offs.

■ ABOVE *Fitting a 145bhp turbocharged engine into the unassuming 99 bodyshell created one of the performance icons of the 1970s.*

Saab pioneered the birth of the popular turbo car with the 99, and it became something of a cult car. Its ruthless turbo speed was quickly duplicated by others such as Audi and many Japanese makers, but none made the formula quite as attractive as Saab.

■ LEFT *Under the forward-hinging bonnet (hood) was Saab turbocharger technology. The Swedish company made the turbo a real speciality.*

SAAB 99 TURBO (1977–80)	
Engine	4-cylinder
Capacity	1985cc
Power	145bhp
Transmission	4-speed manual
Top speed	125mph (201kph)
No. built	10,607

■ ABOVE *The 99 Turbo was angled toward safety: hence the impact (energy-absorbing) bumpers and headlamp wipers.*

■ RIGHT *No one could describe the 99 as a handsome car, but it was utterly unique.*

SUZUKI

■ LEFT *Whizzkid seemed just the right name for Suzuki's tiny sporting projectile. It was an official nickname in Britain.*

■ SUZUKI SC100 WHIZZKID

When your traffic jams are in danger of becoming full-scale preserves, you are forced to do something drastic. The traffic jams of Tokyo and Osaka are the worst in the world, and the Japanese government's solution was to offer tax and parking breaks for owners of very small cars, called K-class cars.

Suzuki was the first company to offer a "K" car (in 1955), and its offerings have always been among the best. One interesting departure was the Cervo of 1972. This was a rare attempt to introduce some zing into the species. It was a two-plus-two coupé based on the rear-engined Suzuki Fronte saloon, measuring just 126in (320cm) long. It used a tiny 539cc two-stroke engine developing 28bhp. Its top speed of 65mph (105kph) was hardly thrilling, but then this was always intended to be a city car first and foremost.

For export Suzuki transformed the Cervo to become the rumbustious SC100 GX, which was known in Britain by its nickname, Whizzkid. The old two-pot engine was replaced by a 970cc four-cylinder Alto engine developing 47bhp, still sited in the tail. Now the little coupé really flew: its top speed jumped

■ ABOVE *The SC100's minute size can be gauged from this shot of one next to a Princess limousine. It was just 10ft 6in (320cm) long.*

■ ABOVE *It was the SC100's narrowness that was surprising to western drivers, but it was designed to conform to Japan's city laws.*

to 85mph (137kph), and there was sparkling acceleration and brilliant fuel economy to match.

It sold for a bargain price, too, and at this level no European maker had ever offered the SC100's lavish list of equipment: rev counter, reclining front seats, cigar lighter, front disc brakes and all-round independent suspension. Suzuki's British importers sold all the cars they could from 1979 to 1982, and now it has minor classic status.

SUZUKI SC100 WHIZZKID (1979–82)	
Engine	4-cylinder
Capacity	970cc
Power	47bhp @ 5000rpm
Transmission	4-speed
Top speed	85mph (137kph)
No. built	894,000 (7,539 UK Whizzkids)

■ FAR LEFT *In action the Whizzkid was a real joy. Its 1.0-litre engine gave it nippy acceleration, but it was dodging through heavy traffic that was most fun.*

■ LEFT *The engine was sited in the tail, making passenger accommodation tight. Giugiaro was responsible for the styling.*

S U Z U K I

■ SUZUKI CAPPUCCINO

If Cappuccino means a hot frothy coffee brew that gives you a lift when you need it, then Suzuki's car truly lived up to the name. The little Cappuccino sportscar began life as a show car in 1989, intended to show what could be done within Japan's "K" class mini-car regulations.

The reaction was so good that Suzuki went into production in early 1992 at the very limited rate of 200 per month. It was a car dedicated to the eccentric Japanese market, but there were still some exports to certain markets such as the UK.

The Cappuccino may have been a tiny car – just 130ins (330cm) long and 55ins (140cm) wide – but it was big on character. The rounded curves were reminiscent of the Austin-Healey Frogeye Sprite. The tail was cut off so

that you could almost stretch out a hand from the cockpit and touch the rear bumper.

The Cappuccino's *pièce de résistance* was its ingenious three-piece folding hardtop roof, which could be put into no less than five positions: fully enclosed; with one targa panel removed, both removed for "T"-bar motoring; all roof panels out but the rear-window section in place, or with the rear part folded down

for the complete open-air treatment.

Considering its 658cc three-cylinder engine, this was a surprisingly rapid little machine: if you removed the 87mph (140kph) top-speed limiter, it was capable of reaching 110mph (177kph) and sprinting from 0–60mph (0–96kph) in about nine seconds. It also handled incredibly well, sounded great and was amazing fun, all for a price that embarrassed any other sportscar.

■ ABOVE *The little Suzuki sportscar was designed around Japanese city car rules – just 130in (330cm) long and 55in (140cm) wide.*

SUZUKI CAPPUCCINO (1992–)

Engine	3-cylinder
Capacity	658cc
Power	64bhp @ 6500rpm
Transmission	5-speed
Top speed	87mph (140kph)
No. built	Still in production

OTHER MAKES

■ SEAT

Spain's only home-grown marque started life as a branch of the Fiat empire in 1953, though it made several models unique to its own market. The most interesting of these was the Sport coupé of 1975–80, a small Fiat 128 3p rival. In the 1980s, Seat shed its Fiat chains and was bought by VW, which developed the marque as its sporty, Latin brand.

■ SKODA

The Czech-made Skoda marque can be traced back to the last century and has an illustrious history. By the 1970s, however, it had become a bit of a joke with its poorly made, wayward-handling rear-engined cars. The 1970–81 S110R coupé was the only vaguely "classic" model, although *Autocar* called the later 136 Rapid a "mini-Porsche". After a take-over by VW, quality and design improved.

■ STUTZ

An American industrialist bought the famous pre-war Stutz name in 1969 and launched a Virgil Exner-styled coupé to revive the long-lost marque. It was based on a Pontiac Grand Prix and was partly made in Italy. The tastefulness of the design might have been questionable but the model hit a chord in Hollywood and Arab markets. Various body styles were offered, including convertibles, saloons (sedans) and a mammoth Royale limousine.

■ SUBARU

Hill farmers loved the Subaru because it combined saloon (sedan) car urbanity with unstoppable four-wheel-drive transmission. Subaru built on this all-wheel-drive reputation with a range of interesting cars, culminating in the curious XT sports coupé, the Legacy saloon and the stunningly fast, rally-winning Impreza Turbo. Quality was always high on the agenda.

TALBOT-SUNBEAM LOTUS

■ TALBOT SUNBEAM LOTUS

"Put a Chrysler Sunbeam in your life" went the glib ad campaign for the new supermini from Chrysler in 1977. Within two years the group had been sold to Peugeot, which renamed all Chrysler models as Talbots, including the Sunbeam.

This thoroughly unexceptional hatchback was based on the Hillman Avenger, but that did engender one strong advantage: unlike most superminis, this model had rear-wheel drive and therefore exploitable handling. In short, it was ripe for a pump up in volume.

So the Sunbeam Lotus was born. Lotus had a history of engineering exciting road cars for mainstream makers (witness the Ford Lotus Cortina), and it did a wonderful job on the Sunbeam. Into the engine bay went Lotus's 2.2-litre twin-cam engine, whose 150bhp made this one of the fastest of the brat pack of rally-orientated specials around at the time: 121mph (195kph) top speed and a 0–60mph (0–96kph) time of 7.4 seconds.

Lotus also specified a five-speed ZF gearbox with first gear canted over to the

left in true racing style. The suspension was lowered and stiffened and brand new wide alloy wheels were created. The live axle and rear drum brakes may not have been very sophisticated but the set-up was certainly effective, as Henri Toivonen found out when he won the World Rally Championship in a Sunbeam Lotus.

The Sunbeam Lotus felt special, too, with its black (later also blue) paint, silver side stripes and prominent Lotus badging. Its career was cut short in 1981 when the plug was pulled on the whole Sunbeam range.

■ LEFT *While the Talbot Sunbeam was an instantly forgettable hatchback, the Sunbeam Lotus was a memorable performance car.*

■ BELOW *The Lotus 2.2 litre twin-cam engine was a comfortable fit. Its 150bhp power output made the Sunbeam the quickest hot hatch around.*

TALBOT SUNBEAM LOTUS (1979–81)	
Engine	4-cylinder
Capacity	2174cc
Power	150bhp
Transmission	5-speed manual
Top speed	121mph (195kph)
No. built	2,308

■ LEFT *In overall terms, the Sunbeam Lotus was highly effective and, because only 2,308 were made, it is now very collectable.*

■ RIGHT *Although it was based closely on the standard Sunbeam, the interior had a special rally-style feel to it.*

TOYOTA

■ TOYOTA CELICA

In Toyota's sprawling range of models, the Celica stands out as a model that has consistently had integrity, style and a certain panache. In the Toyota scheme of things, it has always slotted in as the four-seater coupé model and for the first generations it was based on the Carina saloon (sedan) floorpan.

The first Celica appeared in 1970 with exactly the right balance of Coke-bottle styling and good proportions. For the first three years, the shape was always a notchback, but from 1973 an attractive new Liftback rear-end was also offered.

Various engines were used, the most popular being the 1600 and 2000,

■ LEFT *A Japanese Ford Mustang might be a good description of the first series Toyota Celica coupé.*

■ ABOVE *In Liftback style, the Toyota Celica looked stylish, and it is a rare popular Japanese car with true classic credentials.*

■ ABOVE *Engines offered in the first-generation Celica range from a 1600 OHV up to a 2000 OHC, which developed 130bhp.*

TOYOTA CELICA (1970–77)	
Engine	4-cylinder
Capacity	1407–2289cc
Power	86–130bhp
Transmission	5-speed manual 3-speed auto
Top speed	102–112mph (164–180kph)
No. built	1,500,000

which were available in overhead-valve, overhead-cam and twin-cam forms. The best models were the GT versions with their extra power and sports equipment.

Toyota made sure, in true Japanese style, that every Celica was lavishly equipped. Even the most basic model had five gauges, a cigar lighter and stereo – real luxuries in those days.

The first-generation Celica was

replaced in 1977 by another stylish model, and then again in 1981. In 1985, the fourth-generation Celica became very much more stylish, with its smooth shape, pop-up headlamps and airy cabin, while a convertible version was new to the range. The 1989 edition sold as well as ever, and the Celica – now in its sixth generation – is a much-valued name in the Toyota portfolio.

■ ABOVE *The fifth-generation Celica was controversial in appearance but continued to forge ahead in the sales charts.*

■ RIGHT *This is a fourth-generation Celica, the first to be offered in a convertible body style.*

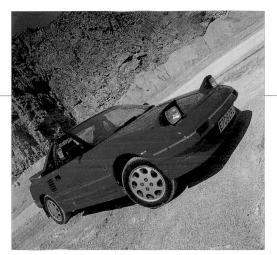

■ LEFT *Nothing less than a miniature Ferrari was how many press writers were unashamed to describe Toyota's brilliant MR2 sportscar.*

■ TOYOTA MR2

Twelve years after the launch of the mid-engined Fiat X1/9, Toyota came up with the first credible rival, the MR2, in 1984. Many expensive and exotic cars used the layout, but on affordable sportscars it had previously been the exclusive province of Fiat and, perhaps, the Pontiac Fiero in America.

MR2 stood for Midships Recreational 2-seater. By plundering the corporate parts bin Toyota created a good-value, sure-fire winner. It had a smooth, responsive twin cam engine matched to immaculate mid-engined poise, a combination nobody could touch in the affordable sportscar arena. If traditionalists were suspicious of the slightly bland angular styling – not to mention Toyota's questionable pedigree as a maker of exciting cars – then one drive around the block in the 120mph (193kph), 30mpg (48kpg) MR2 would almost certainly win them over.

Without doubt this was a very special car, justifying its reputation as a "mini-Ferrari". To keep its appeal broad Toyota made sure the MR2 rode like a saloon (sedan), was acceptably quiet and had a saloon-car driving position, not a low-slung sporty one that might have been off-putting. About the only black mark was the lack of cockpit space.

From 1986 there was a T-bar version with a removable roof section. In Japan, there was an even more exciting 145bhp supercharged model, but that was not imported to Europe because it would only run on unleaded fuel. It was sold in North America however, and there was a rather dull single-cam model for the home market.

The original MR2 has inspired two more generations of mid-engined Toyotas – and indeed Britain's mid-engined MGF – and looks set to become a sportscar classic of the next century.

■ LEFT *The MR2 badge came to mean everything enjoyable in handling terms.*

■ ABOVE *Thanks to its mid-mounted engine, the MR2 had not only sporting performance but also balance and poise.*

■ ABOVE *The standard 1.6-litre engine developed 130bhp and was sited, crucially, amidships.*

■ ABOVE *A new-generation MR2 replaced the squarish first series in 1989, expanded both in size and appeal.*

TOYOTA MR2 (1984–89)	
Engine	4-cylinder
Capacity	1587cc
Power	130bhp @ 6600rpm
Transmission	5-speed manual
Top speed	120mph (193kph)
No. built	166,104

TRIUMPH

■ TRIUMPH DOLOMITE SPRINT

The Triumph brand could be described as the BMW of the British car industry, since its strength lay in creating high-quality saloons (sedans) and sportscars with appeal for the enthusiastic driver. No other car summed this up so well as the Dolomite Sprint.

It was the engine that set the Sprint apart from most other British saloons of the 1970s; 16-valve technology was unusual in 1973, and Triumph's overhead-cam unit pioneered 16V technology two decades before it became *de rigueur*. The engine was simple, retaining a single chain-driven camshaft – and the design was so clever that it won a Design Council Award in 1974.

Certainly the engine was punchy and effective: 0–60mph (0–96kph) in under nine seconds was blistering for a saloon car in 1973, and embarrassed many so-called sportscars such as the MGB. The parent company, British Leyland, was keen to promote its sporting image and entered it for many races; a Sprint won the British Saloon Car Championships of

■ ABOVE *Triumph was a name associated with high-quality sporting saloons (sedans), and its Dolomite Sprint was the best of them all.*

■ LEFT *The 16-valve head on top of the 2.0-litre engine was ahead of its time in 1973, allowing 127bhp.*

TRIUMPH DOLOMITE SPRINT (1973–80)	
Engine	4-cylinder
Capacity	1998cc
Power	127bhp @ 5700rpm
Transmission	4-speed manual 3-speed auto
Top speed	115mph (186kph)
No. built	22,941

■ LEFT *The Dolomite Sprint lasted until 1980, and there was no direct replacement for its combination of rear-drive handling, keen performance and classic style.*

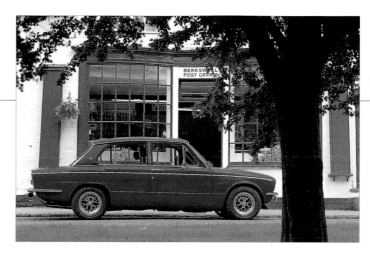

■ RIGHT *Italian stylist Michelotti was responsible for the stylish shape, even though it looked a little outdated by the mid-1970s.*

1975 and 1978, and many rallying successes were also scored.

The four-speed gearbox was derived from the TR6 and could be had with optional overdrive (standard from 1975). Alternatively, you could choose an automatic (which was very rare, with only 1,634 built). Other significant changes over the standard-issue Toledo/Dolomite were larger brakes,

■ RIGHT *In handling terms the Sprint was very sharp around corners, yet it was equally at home cruising down the motorway.*

■ ABOVE *Conservative in style, the interior was a rather messy array of classic dials in a wood facia.*

twin headlamps, a vinyl roof, front spoiler and alloy wheels (the first time any British production car had boasted these as standard).

The Dolomite Sprint had a rounded character. It was rapid and urgent when pressed, yet refined and relaxed when cruising in overdrive top. The handling was sharp at all times, mild understeer transferring into power oversteer if you provoked the car around bends.

The character of the interior was typically British: a full-width wood dashboard, hard-wearing trim and a profusion of traditional gauges.

Overheating, head gasket problems and poor-quality control marred an otherwise brilliant car. Also, it was poorly timed, being launched just as the Arab–Israeli conflict forced petrol shortages in Britain, and thirsty cars like the Dolomite Sprint fell out of favour.

An interesting Dolly Sprint variant was the 1975 Panther Rio built by a British specialist. This was a real mini-Rolls-Royce with hand-beaten replacement panels and a leather-and-walnut luxury interior. However, at three times the price of the Dolomite Sprint, only a handful were ever made.

■ RIGHT *Thanks to its advanced engine, the Sprint was a real performer; a 115mph (186kph) top speed was very healthy for a small saloon.*

When the Dolomite left production in 1980, that was sadly the end of the line for old-style Triumphs, and on the death of the model the Canley and Speke plants that had made it were closed. The following year the Honda-based Acclaim scotched any remaining pride in the marque, and it died three years later.

TRIUMPH

■ TRIUMPH TR7/TR8

The long line of TR-badged Triumph sports cars stretches back to the TR2 of the early 1950s and boasts some of the most charismatic sporting machines among its family. For many the ultimate TR7 was the runt of the litter, a quirky, unappealing product of the depressing British Leyland years of the 70s.

Certainly the TR7 was controversially styled: its lines were penned by Harris Mann (who also has the Austin Allegro to his credit). Build quality was never up to much: they tended to break down and catch fire, and the fixed-head model in

particular had very little appeal. Yet there is much to be said in favour of the maligned TR7. It sold in greater quantity than any other TR model, and in due course it became a rather attractive sportscar, at least in convertible form.

The original plan had been to make a drop-top TR7, but concerns about American legislation possibly banning open cars led Triumph to launch the new sportscar in fixed-head form only in 1975. For lovers of the machismo of Triumph TR straight-six power disappointment lurked, for British Leyland opted to fit a mere four-cylinder

■ LEFT *TR8 models were quite rare and much sought-after by aficionados.*

■ ABOVE *The TR7 enjoyed some success in rallying. With a V-eight engine in place, it was undoubtedly the quickest rally car around.*

■ RIGHT *With age the TR7 matured into a much better car. Sadly, the 16-valve Dolomite Sprint engine never made it into a production TR7.*

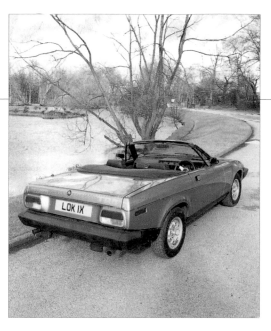

engine (the 105bhp Dolomite 1850 unit),
driving through a Morris Marina four
speed gearbox. It was frankly not a
sporting package at all.

Despite this, export sales went pretty
well, especially in America (British sales
did not begin until May 1976). Some of
the criticisms were addressed with the
adoption of a Rover SD1 five-speed
gearbox in 1976 and lowered suspension
the following year. But it was not until
the drop-top model was added in 1979
that the TR7 turned the corner and
became a real sportscar.

Still there was not enough power for
many tastes. Triumph fitted its fine twin-
cam Dolomite Sprint engine to its rally
cars, but road cars were denied this
option. Instead a stunning Rover V-eight-
powered version was offered for export

■ LEFT *The TR8 is
regarded as the
poor relation of
Triumph sportscars
and is often derided.
It did, however,
become a true
sportscar, and its day
as a classic will
surely dawn soon.*

■ BELOW *With a
Rover V-eight engine
fitted, the TR7
became the TR8
and made some
inroads into the
American market.*

■ ABOVE *The interior was a typical 1970s
concoction of black plastic. The drop-top
looked particularly neat when folded.*

TRIUMPH TR7/TR8 (1975–81)	
Engine	4/V-eight-cylinder
Capacity	1998/3528cc
Power	105/137bhp
Transmission	4/5-speed manual 3-speed auto
Top speed	110–120mph (177–193kph)
No. built	112,368

only, dubbed the TR8. This model was
actually quite rare (only 2,497 were
made) and soon private owners were
doing their own V-eight installations on
TR7s, a fad that assumed epidemic
proportions since the performance was so
much better: 137bhp in "soft" tune
meant 120mph (193kph) instead of
110mph (177kph) and 0–60mph
(0–96kph) in 8.4 seconds. These figures
could be greatly enhanced by tuning the
V-eight engine to even higher levels.

Production finally ended in 1981,
and few enthusiasts mourned the death
of the TR7; far more sad for them
was that this event marked the demise
of the great Triumph sportscar. The
TR7 was a car that never fulfilled
its potential but which has recently
started to gain a following. Its
distinctive style and bargain prices
make it a surprisingly attractive
sportscar and a sure-fire candidate
for future classic status.

TVR

■ TVR 3000S

TVR is one of those very British specialist car-makers, producing highly individual sportscars against all odds of success. The company's convoluted history goes back as far as 1947, and by the late 1970s it was firmly established as an iconic sportscar-maker.

The 3000S was the ultimate expression of a line of TVR sportscars stretching back to the 1957 Grantura. The TVR formula was very traditional: a separate chassis, glassfibre body, Ford V-six engine and luxuriously trimmed cabin. However, the idea of a convertible was new to TVR, and the 1978 "S" was its very first drop-top.

Based closely on a one-off produced for TVR boss Martin Lilley, the 3000S shared most of its specification with the fixed-head TVR 3000M Taimar, including the chassis and mechanicals. The bodywork was much lower, the doors were new and the tail was revised to incorporate a boot (trunk) lid. The lower scuttle line (hood line) also forced the instruments to be repositioned, with the rev counter (tachometer) now facing the passenger! Another traditional-style feature was removable soft side screens.

■ LEFT An original 1978 3000S sits in front of a pair of revived S models, which were launched in 1986.

■ BELOW After more than 20 years, TVR's first convertible model was the 3000S, based on the 3000M seen in the background.

TVR 3000S (1978–79)	
Engine	V-six-cylinder
Capacity	2994cc
Power	142–265bhp
Transmission	4-speed
Top speed	133–150mph (214–241kph)
No. built	258

■ ABOVE Proving that the formula of a good-value, open-topped two-seater sportscar never died, TVR made a relaunched S model from 1986 until the mid-1990s.

The 3000S lasted for just one year, when a brand-new model range took over. In that time, a mere 258 cars were made, including 13 turbocharged cars. The 3000S Turbo is the most classic of all the earlier TVRs, having incredible performance and rarity on its side. The S was so sorely missed that in 1986 TVR relaunched it in revised form.

■ ABOVE In character and form, the 3000S recalled the great days of British rag-top roadsters like the Austin-Healey 3000.

■ ABOVE In action, the TVR was keen thanks to its Ford-derived V-six engine. With an optional turbocharger, it became a brutal machine.

■ RIGHT *With the Cerbera, TVR took a bold new direction in 1994. Here was its first two-plus-two model for a decade, its first all-new engine ever, and its most sophisticated project ever.*

■ TVR CERBERA

The Cerbera, named after a creature from classical mythology, was first seen at the 1994 Birmingham Motor Show. The long, low two-plus-two coupé may have drawn on other TVR models for its styling inspiration, but the outcome was the best model TVR had ever produced.

TVR's dynamic approach to design meant that, from debut to production readiness, the Cerbera took little over two years. Especially challenging was the all-new AJP V-eight engine, the first engine designed and developed entirely by TVR. It was initially used in racing TVR Tuscans but was refined enough to pass tough emissions tests. Like all other power plants used in TVRs, the AJP sounded raw and urgent, yet was also remarkably smooth.

The 4.2-litre engine developed a monstrous 350bhp and could rev as high as 7000rpm. Unencumbered by aerodynamic weakness, the Cerbera was capable of staggering performance: 0–60mph (0–96kph) in 4.0 seconds and up to 185mph (298kph) top speed. An even more thunderous 4.5-litre GT version was shown in 1996 – it had no less than 440bhp.

The Cerbera's chassis was quite capable of dealing with all that power. Its handling was safe yet exploitable and fun, while the ride quality was firm yet comfortable.

Undoubtedly one of the car's best features was its interior. The cabin was a haven of curves, which were almost sci-fi in the way their loops swathed the passengers – all four of them, at a push. The leather-stitched console incorporated classy black-on-white dials, while the underslung cluster of dials below the steering wheel worked very well. The Cerbera has become a fitting top-of-the-range model in TVR's line-up.

■ LEFT *The muscular, almost hot-rod appearance was widely admired, and neat details like the hidden electric door "handles" made it unique.*

■ BELOW *Not only was the design work stunning, the new Cerbera was one of the fastest cars of its day: 185mph (298kph) from TVR's AJP V-eight engine.*

TVR CERBERA (1996–)	
Engine	V-eight-cylinder
Capacity	4185cc
Power	350bhp @ 6500rpm
Transmission	5-speed
Top speed	185mph (298kph)
No. built	Still in production

■ ABOVE *The interior was equally innovative. The sculpted dashboard looked fabulous and the siting of an instrument cluster under the steering column worked very well.*

T V R

■ TVR GRIFFITH

TVR progressed into the 1980s with a
new chairman at the helm, businessman
and true enthusiast of the marque Peter
Wheeler, who succeeded in turning
TVR's fortunes around in no uncertain
terms. Wheeler quickly realized what
his customers wanted and concentrated
his efforts on making convertible two-
seaters with glassfibre bodies and
brawny Rover V-eight engines.

The angular Tasmin series of
1980–91 was successful, if not exactly
pretty, but the car it led to was
undeniably a masterstroke. The Griffith
had its roots in the TVR Tuscan racer

■ ABOVE *Power slides were part and parcel
of the Griffith package. With 280bhp on tap
and no traction control system, care was
always required.*

■ LEFT *The Griffith marked a radical break
away from TVR's past into a bold and highly
successful future. Mature styling and
increasingly powerful V-eight engines
headed the move.*

first seen in 1988, which used the
familiar TVR tubular chassis, uprated
suspension and a monster 400bhp V-
eight engine. Tuscans were raced in one
of the quickest and most exciting one-
make series in the world but were never
officially homologated for road use.

The spirit of the Tuscan resurfaced in
the new Griffith, a pukka road-going car
launched at the Birmingham Motor
Show in 1990, but not actually available
until late 1991. The Griffith name
harked back to the magnificently hairy
Ford V-eight powered TVRs of the mid-

1960s. The justification for exploiting
that heritage was certainly there, since
the first edition of the new Griffith
sported a V-eight engine based on the
unit still used in the Range Rover, and
developing either 240bhp or 280bhp.

In looks, the Griffith was far removed
from TVRs of old: instead of angular
and slightly gawky lines there were
swoopy curves everywhere, a profile
unbroken by styling adornments and
clever air ducting at the leading edges of
the bonnet (hood) and doors. Other neat
styling details included a lack of

■ ABOVE *Few other cars could match the
character of the Griffith's leather-and-wood
sculpted interior.*

■ LEFT *In a Griffith 500 you could screech away from rest to 60mph (96 kph) in just over four seconds. This was an old-school macho sportscar for the modern age.*

exterior door handles, evocative aluminium knobs in the cabin and a removable solid centre roof section. Perhaps the most impressive aspect of the Griffith was that it was almost totally designed and produced in-house. Considering the brilliance of the end product, this was a remarkable achievement for such a small size company.

Testers were immediately impressed by the Griffith's character: an almost forgotten formula of raw V-eight power, rear wheel drive and a rich, burbling exhaust note that was like no other car. Some even compared its overall impact to that of the E-Type Jaguar in 1961, since the TVR offered a similarly intoxicating brew of luscious curves, superior performance and exceptional value for money. No other sportscar offered so much for so little, and TVR grew in size and importance on the back of Griffith sales.

If the press was impressed with the Griffith, it was rapturous about the 1993 Griffith 500, whose engine grew in size to five litres and which developed no less than 345bhp. Now you could expect

■ RIGHT *The powerful Griffith boasted one of the greatest exhaust notes in motoring.*

a 0–60mph (0–96kph) time of a little over four seconds and mid-range punch and low-speed torque the like of which was simply not available elsewhere.

TVR followed up the Griffith with other models such as the cheaper Chimaera and even more potent Cerbera, but neither had the impact of the original, svelte Griffith, which remains one of the most popular models in the Blackpool manufacturer's repertoire.

TVR GRIFFITH (1990–)	
Engine	V-eight-cylinder
Capacity	3947–4997cc
Power	243–345bhp
Transmission	5-speed
Top speed	152–163mph (245–262kph)
No. built	Still in production

■ LEFT *The gauges had to be recalibrated in a Griffith to suit its phenomenal performance – up to 163mph (262kph) top speed. Cabin architecture was widely admired in TVRs.*

■ ABOVE *The innocuous-seeming "500" tag on the end of the Griffith name hinted at its new 5.0-litre V-eight engine and its 345bhp of raw power.*

VAUXHALL

■ VAUXHALL LOTUS CARLTON

In March 1989, news filtered through that Vauxhall was cooperating with Lotus in the development of a high-performance version of the Carlton saloon (sedan) (known as the Opel Omega outside Britain). When it became clear that General Motors was not going to follow the lead set by BMW and Mercedes-Benz in limiting top speed to 155mph (249kph), a minor media storm broke out. The new Lotus Carlton, said the press, was irresponsible: its top speed of 176mph (283kph) was more than anyone should ever be doing.

The controversy over the Lotus Carlton's speed was spurious. Any number of cars from Porsche, Ferrari or Aston Martin were capable of going much faster than this. The germ of the problem in the media's eyes was that the Carlton was a family car, capable of seating four adults in comfort. In practice, this was the Lotus Carlton's unique selling point, since no other supercar could transport so many so fast. In truth, it was all a storm in the proverbial teacup, since the volume of

■ ABOVE *A four-seater saloon (sedan) with a Vauxhall badge that was capable of 176mph (283kph) – it could only be the Lotus Carlton.*

■ LEFT *The prominent Lotus badging betrayed the work done to this 3.6-litre six-cylinder engine, which developed 377bhp.*

VAUXHALL LOTUS CARLTON (1989–92)	
Engine	6-cylinder
Capacity	3615cc
Power	377bhp @ 5200rpm
Transmission	6-speed manual
Top speed	176mph (283kph)
No. built	440

■ LEFT *Apart from a body kit, rear spoiler and five-spoke alloy wheels, this could have been any member of the rather ordinary Carlton/Omega family.*

cars sold was tiny, General Motors wanted to sell 1,100, but, in fact, only 440 were built because of the effects of the recession on sales.

The heart of the new supersaloon was its Lotus-developed 3.6-litre six-cylinder 24-valve engine. With its twin turbochargers, catalysts and advanced electronic management, it had huge power and torque. This, together with a Corvette ZR-1 six-speed gearbox, gave performance that was simply sensational. The Carlton accelerated faster than a Ferrari Testarossa and could reach 160mph (256kph) in under a mile.

Not only did it go fast in a straight line, it cornered and stopped with great finesse – a car with the Lotus badge on it should behave in no other way. Self-levelling dampers controlled the suspension superbly, providing handling of an order that belied the car's bulk. *Autocar* magazine described the braking as "the best we've tried on a road car".

Far from being a nervous, temperamental sportscar, the Lotus Carlton was benign and extremely safe. It would happily idle around town and was forgiving if abused. You could also go

shopping, since the boot was huge – and the rear seats folded to increase capacity.

Passengers were supremely cosseted. You got leather seats, a leather steering wheel, polished wood and pleated cloth trim, plus head restraints all round, six-speaker CD hi-fi, air-conditioning, electric windows and a sunroof. The

Lotus Carlton looked the part too. Its body kit comprised a deep front spoiler, wheel-arch extensions, aerodynamic side skirts, a new rear bumper and a boot spoiler; and there was just one colour, Imperial Green. The price was certainly high at £48,000 ($80,840) but entirely justified by the car's rarity and specification.

■ LEFT *As well as being exceedingly quick, the Lotus Carlton was fun around corners and extremely safe into the bargain.*

■ LEFT *Apart from the Lotus badging, 180mph (290kph) speedometer and extra electrical equipment, this could have been an ordinary saloon (sedan) car dashboard.*

■ ABOVE *This was a very comfortably trimmed car, with standard leather, polished wood and a host of equipment.*

■ RIGHT *In the tail-pipes of the Lotus Carlton was a whiff of the political controversy that surrounded its high top speed.*

VOLKSWAGEN

■ VOLKSWAGEN GOLF GTI

Based on the best supermini the mid-
1970s had to offer, the VW Golf GTI was
the father of the modern hot-hatch brat-
pack, setting the standards for two
generations to come. When the first Golf
GTI appeared in 1975, who could have
guessed that production figures would
pass 1.35 million by the time the car
reached its 20th birthday? Certainly not
Volkswagen itself, which only envisaged a
short run of 5,000 units for the sporty
hatchback in those gloomy years
following the fuel crisis.

The first prototypes were fitted with
the 80bhp carburettor engine from the
Audi 80 GT, but by the time the car
appeared at the 1975 Frankfurt Motor
Show it was sporting fuel injection for an
output of 110bhp. The first model had a
four-speed gearbox driving through the
front wheels.

Outwardly there was very little to
mark the GTI out from the standard Golf:
discreet badging, side stripes, a chin

■ BELOW *At first, the Golf GTI was considered
a low-volume production special, but as the
years progressed drivers recognized its
greatness and bought it in huge volumes.*

■ ABOVE *Apart from the subtlest of spoilers
and very minor trim differences, the GTI
looked like a standard hatchback – the
ultimate in understatement.*

spoiler and plastic wheel-arch lips. The
car was an instant hit, mixing punchy
performance and tenacious knock-about
handling from the firmed-up strut
suspension with the practicality of a
well-built three-door hatchback body of
well proven durability. Production
figures leapt from just over 10,000 in
1976 to 31,000 in 1977 and an amazing
42,000 in 1978.

The first right-hand-drive cars were
not launched until July 1979, and that
year multi-spoke BBS alloy wheels and
a five-speed gearbox became part of the
specification. There was a popular
cabriolet version of the GTI, but the
handling suffered from the extra weight
involved in the strengthening of the Golf
shell. The drop-top MkI body shape
lasted right up until 1992.

The best of the MkI GTIs was the 1800 model, replacing the 1600 in 1982. Power went up only marginally, but there was 8lb ft (10.8Nm) of extra torque, produced 1500rpm lower down. You could spot an 1800 by its new wider alloys, twin headlights and steel sunroof.

The GTI has lived through two generations since the demise of the MkI in 1985. The shape has been gradually rounded-off and the power – and luxury – increased. The 16-valvers of the mid-1980s packed 139bhp and came complete with electric windows, sunroof, central locking and driver's seat height adjustment. The facelifted 1990-model-year cars had deeper spoilers and power steering. The most coveted of all the MkIIs is the Rallye, a 5,000-off limited edition four-wheel-drive Golf using VW's Syncro system allied to a 1756cc supercharged engine. Built as a homologation special for rallying, the Rallye spawned the front-drive but supercharged G60. This was built on normal GTI production lines – unlike the Rallye, which was produced in Belgium.

The concept continued in the MkIII Golf, either as a 155bhp 2.0-litre or the blockbuster 140mph (225kph) VR6 complete with super sweet 2.8-litre V-six power – and that is a guaranteed future classic.

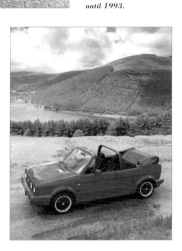

■ LEFT *Available only as a three-door hatchback, the GTI was every bit as useful as a shopping car as for hacking around country roads.*

■ BELOW *The MkI convertible body style lasted right up until 1993.*

VW GOLF GTI MK1 (1975-85)	
Engine	4-cylinder
Capacity	1588–1781cc
Power	110–112bhp
Transmission	4/5-speed manual
Top speed	115mph (185kph)
No. built	350,000

■ LEFT *As a convertible, the GTI caught the mood of the 1980s, even if ultimately it was not as sharp-handling or rigid as the saloon.*

■ ABOVE *As a lightweight car with a powerful 1.6 or 1.8-litre engine, the GTI was a stormer, and its leech-like behaviour around twisty bends won it many friends.*

VOLKSWAGEN

■ VOLKSWAGEN SCIROCCO/CORRADO

Having relied on the rear-engined Beetle and various derivatives for four decades, Volkswagen underwent a complete revolution in the 1970s. It followed the lead taken by its sister company Audi in adopting front engines and front-wheel drive, completely renewing its model range and revitalizing its prospects.

The first of the new generation was the 1973 Passat, the most significant was the 1974 Golf, but the best was the Scirocco, launched two months before the Golf. The Scirocco was developed alongside the Golf and shared many common elements: platform, power trains, suspension and so on. Yet the Scirocco had style, and it also had clarity of purpose as an enjoyable coupé.

Italy's Giugiaro did a superb design job according to the folded-paper school of design. The shape was crisp, taut and light, and the rising glass line was utterly distinctive. For Volkswagen, the Scirocco was a specialist car, so it asked Stuttgart-based firm Karmann to build it. There was a large range of models, starting with

■ RIGHT *The second-generation Scirocco was styled in-house by VW and perhaps lost some of the Giugiaro charm of the first series.*

■ RIGHT *The first-generation Scirocco was like a sharp-suited coupé version of the Golf, and in GTI form became a performance icon.*

lowly 1100 and 1300 versions (though these were not widely exported). Far more satisfying were the larger-engined 1500 and 1600, but the best of all were the models powered by the 110bhp Golf GTI engine. These were variously badged GLI, GTI and Storm and became minor icons of performance motoring, not surprisingly with a top speed of

114mph (183kph) and a 0–60mph (0–96kph) time of 8.9 seconds. The Scirocco was an even better handling car than the Golf.

Automatic transmission was optional on all but the base models and the GTI engined versions. Four-speed manual was standard, although the very last 110bhp models got five speeds as

■ LEFT *All Scirocco models offered keen driving manners with a healthy dose of both style and practicality.*

■ ABOVE *The 1985 16V version of the Scirocco was quite a stormer, having 139bhp at its disposal.*

■ RIGHT *The GTX was a 111bhp mid-range model with a sporting close-ratio five-speed gearbox.*

standard. In 1981 an all-new Scirocco was launched, although to many it was a retrograde step. It had a blander profile, disappointing ride and handling.

Officially the 1989 Corrado was not a replacement for the Scirocco, which was perhaps auspicious because it was a far better car in all respects. The shape returned to the sharp, compact purposefulness of the original Scirocco, but it was underneath where the most impressive work had been done.

Put simply, the Corrado had one of the best front-wheel-drive chassis ever made. Neither the standard 136bhp 1.8-litre engine nor the supercharged 160bhp G60 engine did it justice; drivers had to wait until the 1992 VR6, with its blistering 190bhp 2.8-litre V-six engine, to exploit the chassis to the full: it was fluid, composed, controlled and extremely quick. By the time Corrado production finished in 1995, VW had made half a million.

■ ABOVE *With one of the best front-wheel-drive chassis ever, the Corrado was capable of stunning speeds around corners and, with the right engine, in a straight line, too.*

VOLKSWAGEN SCIROCCO MK1 (1974–80)	
Engine	4-cylinder
Capacity	1093–1588cc
Power	50–110bhp
Transmission	4/5-speed manual 3-speed auto
Top speed	89–114mph (143–183kph)
No. built	504,200

■ ABOVE *The Corrado was altogether a step up: every department had been improved.*

■ RIGHT *Fast, responsive, well-built and very good value, the Scirocco was a bestseller throughout the 1970s and 80s.*

VOLVO

■ VOLVO C70

Volvo design chief Paul Horbury said that he knew he had succeeded with the new C70 when he parked an example outside a prominent Californian hotel, and the valet attendants left it there for show rather than parking it in the parking lot underground.

Volvo's image in the 1970s and 80s was one of staid dreariness. The C70 was symptomatic of the company's turn-around. For its first sports coupé since the '60s it formed a co-venture with UK-based TWR (which engineered the chassis) and the result was the most desirable Volvo ever.

■ ABOVE *With the C70, Sweden's leading car-maker entered new territory, doing battle with Mercedes and BMW coupés.*

■ ABOVE *The extremely handsome design of the C70 was penned by Volvo's British-born design chief Paul Horbury.*

■ RIGHT *In full convertible form, the C70 was yet another new departure for Volvo: never before had it offered a series (production) drop-top model.*

VOLVO C70 (1996–)	
Engine	5-cylinder
Capacity	2319–2435cc
Power	193–240bhp
Transmission	5-speed manual 4-speed auto
Top speed	137–146mph (220–235kph)
No. built	Still in production

The C70 borrowed much of its technology from the 850R saloon (sedan), including its 240bhp turbocharged five-cylinder engine driving the front wheels. Since it was lighter and more aerodynamic, the C70 posted even better performance figures than the 850R: 146mph (235kph) top speed and 0–60mph (0–96kph) in 6 7 seconds.

The cabin reflected functional Scandinavian themes, with a huge choice of colour schemes and tasteful, luxurious decoration. The ten-speaker

■ ABOVE *Volvo's new executive-class coupé looked like a convincing alternative to the best coupés in its class.*

■ ABOVE *Described as "typically Swedish", the C70 interior was a paragon of tasteful luxury. Full four-seater convertibles have always been rarities.*

hi-fi was among the best available anywhere in the world. Even more attractive than the coupé was the full convertible version announced shortly afterwards at the 1997 Geneva Motor Show.

The C70 secured a starring role in the Hollywood film *The Saint* starring Val Kilmer. Through the TWR connection, two of the first "customers" for the new Volvo were Formula 1 racers Damon Hill and Pedro Diniz, who both received a C70 as personal transport.

■ RIGHT *Even with its hood (top) raised, the C70 managed to look aristocratic and stylish.*

INDEX

NOTES

NOTES

NOTES

NOTES